SAINT PETER LIVES

IN ROME

Saint Peter Lives in Rome

An Anglican Discovers the Ministry of the Pope

Robert A. Stackpole, STD
Director of the John Paul II Institute of Divine Mercy
Professor of Theology, Redeemer Pacific College

John Paul II Institute of Divine Mercy

An Imprint of Marian Press
2005

Nihil Obstat:
Rev. Richard J. Drabik, M.I.C.
Provincial Censor
July 2, 2004

Imprimi Potest:
Very Rev. Walter M. Dziordz, M.I.C., D. Min.
Provincial Superior

Library of Congress Catalog Number: 2004115196

ISBN: 1-59614-112-3

Typesetting: *Marina Batiuk*
Cover Design: *William Sosa*

Front Cover: Saint Peter's at the Vatican in Rome and the keys of the
office of St. Peter.

Published by:
John Paul II Institute of Divine Mercy
An imprint of *Marian Press*

Marians of the Immaculate Conception
Stockbridge, Massachusetts 01262

*For Katherine
and Christina*

TABLE OF CONTENTS

Introduction 9

I. The Ministry of St. Peter in Holy Scripture 13

The Scriptural Evidence..13

Alternative Theories: "Liberal" Scholarship 16

Alternative Theories: Evangelical and Orthodox.............22

The Petrine Ministry...30

Petrine Succession 33

II. The Petrine Ministry in the Patristic Era 38

Other New Testament Models of the Church....................40

The Petrine Primacy and the City of Rome 49

The Witness of St. Ireneus and St. Leo the Great 52

The Ancient Consensus 58

The Consensus in the East 60

The Consensus in the West...71

The Rise of Constantinople 73

III.The Universal Jurisdiction
     of the Successors of St. Peter 78

The Challenge of St. Cyprian...81

The Scope of Universal Jurisdiction 83

Not an "Absolute Monarchy" 88

Misgivings of a Convert 93

IV. The Infallibility of the Successors of St. Peter 100

The Scriptural Foundation 101

A Fanciful Spectre 107

The "Rationalist" and "Modernist" Challenge................111

Universal Reception: An Eastern
and Anglican Challenge 115

Papal Infallibility: Infallibly Defined?............................121

V. The Petrine Ministry:
   Yesterday, Today and Tomorrow 126

Yesterday: A Fallible Papacy? 126

Today and Tomorrow 135

Postscript: An Olive Branch from the East? 144

A Truncated History...145

An Idealistic Ecclesiology 153

Toward Re-union 158

INTRODUCTION

This little book is a brief attempt to address the most contentious issue in Christian ecumenical dialogue: the role of the papacy in Christ's holy Church. As a matter of fact, it is written by a theologian who was once something of an ecumenical wanderer himself. Born the son of a Protestant pastor, I became an Anglican as an undergraduate, and later pursued a vocation to the Anglican priesthood. I will always be sincerely grateful for all that I learned about God and His love, and about His Son Jesus Christ, through the years of my Protestant upbringing and Anglican formation.

Nevertheless, I always felt that something important was missing from what had been given to me. Several times, I *almost* became a Catholic — a sign of my inner restlessness — but then drew back. The distinctive Roman Catholic doctrines about Mary, the saints, purgatory, and the Eucharist were never the most serious stumbling blocks for me (after all, I could accept all those doctrines and remain a "High" Anglican, or even become Eastern Orthodox). It was the doctrine of the papacy, the Petrine Ministry, which really stood in the way.

After much prayer and study, I found it no longer stood in the way. This book explains why.

Sadly, I know from the outset that many readers of this book will be very disappointed by what I have to say. I would guess that what many would *want* me to write, what they would *hope* I would write, is that from a Catholic perspective, there is an ever increasing possibility for ecumenical reconciliation among the Christian churches regarding the proper role of the papacy.

Sadly, I do not believe that to be the case. To be sure, we are much closer together on this issue than we were a century ago. One can certainly try to clarify the dogmatic foundations of the papacy in Scripture, Tradition and Reason. All this I will try to do, from a Catholic perspective, in the chapters that follow.

In the end, however, I believe sincere Christians are still faced with a *choice* to make. This is not one of those issues which can be dismissed after much careful study, as a mere ecumenical misunderstanding, or semantic disagreement. Nor can it be relegated to the area of dogmatic inessentials. As the whole history of the Church shows, the unity of the Body of Christ, and the means our Lord has given to us to secure that unity in truth and love, are vital and essential to the whole mission of the Church. Christian unity is not an "optional-extra" to the Church's mission; rather, it is the supreme manifestation of the grace of Christ in the world, without which the task of evangelism is largely crippled. Jesus Himself taught us this in St. John's gospel, chapters 10 and 17:

> And I have other sheep, that are not of this fold; I must bring them also, and they will heed my voice. So there shall be one flock, one shepherd (10:16).

> I do not pray for these only, but also for those who believe in me through their word, that they all may be one; even as thou, Father, art in me, and I in thee, that they also may be one in us, so that the world may believe that thou hast sent me (17:20-23).

Commenting on these passages, the Catholic apologist Stephen Ray has pointed out:

> A sheepfold provides a distinct enclosure whereby the sheep are protected, kept together, and fed. ... Jesus never meant the Church to be rent by divisions, torn asunder into competing denominations and sects. He prayed that the Church, his flock, would be one and perfected in unity. This cannot be relegated to an "invisible" unity, for only a visible and organic unity can be seen and observed by the world ["that they may all be one ... so that the world may believe ..."] [1]

I trust that all Christians, whatever church body we may belong to at present, believe in Jesus Christ as Lord and Saviour. All of us want to accept everything that God has revealed to us through Him, and want to follow Him with faith and love. This is our great and inspired "common ground," and thanks be to God that in our ecumenical age we finally recognize that fact, and can pray together, and cooperate in many areas, more than ever before.

Again, all of us want to accept Jesus Christ as our Lord and Saviour, to believe what He reveals, and to follow wherever He leads. But I have become ever more convinced that to do so fully, completely and unreservedly, means to do so *in communion with, and in obedience to, His Vicar on earth, in the See of St. Peter.*

This is not "triumphalism"; nor does anyone want to impose this dogma on anyone else. In fact, the 16th century theologian who helped clarify this aspect of Catholic teaching, St. Robert Bellarmine, was himself one of the early advocates for true religious tolerance. What we are up against here is not "triumphalism," but a *definitive conviction:* a conviction that has always, implicitly or explicitly,

---

[1] Stephen K. Ray, *Upon This Rock* (San Francisco: Ignatius Press, 1999), 45.

defined and distinguished the great Catholic Church throughout the world. You may come to hold this conviction someday, or you may not. Whatever you and I decide, of course, must always be done with prayer and charity, as Christ Jesus bids us to do in all things. My task in these chapters is to present to you, as clearly as I can, the teaching of the Catholic Church regarding the papal ministry, to help you make an informed and prayerful *choice.* Certainly I hope and pray that your choice will not be based on my paltry presentation alone — and I doubt, in any case that it would. My task is but to clear away misunderstandings, to clarify foundations, and to explain as best I can, why Catholics hold this "definitive conviction."

Robert Stackpole

I. THE MINISTRY OF ST. PETER IN HOLY SCRIPTURE

For Catholic Christians, everything that God has revealed to us that pertains in any way to the process of our "salvation" — that is, to our growth in the knowledge and love of Him — comes to us through His Son, Jesus Christ. Jesus is God's own "Word," His self-revelation to all the world (Jn. 1:14). This revelation, "the faith which was once and for all delivered to the saints" (Jude: 3), was given by Christ to His apostles, then passed down by the apostles to future generations in two ways: orally (by preaching) and in written form. That is why St. Paul wrote to the earliest Christian communities: "Stand firm and hold to the traditions which you were taught by us, either by word of mouth or by letter" (2 Thess. 2:15). It follows that, if it was really the intention of Jesus Christ, the Son of God, to establish a ministry in His Church like the papacy, we would expect to find clear indications of this both in the writings of the apostles (which are found in the Bible in the New Testament) and in the oral teaching tradition (evidence of which is found in the writings of the early Fathers and saints of the Church, as well as in the ancient liturgies, creeds, and church council documents).

Let us look first at the New Testament.

The Scriptural Evidence

Catholic teaching about the primacy of Peter among the apostles is firmly rooted in the New Testament. From their very first meeting, our Lord singled out Simon by giving him a new name: Cephas, or Peter, "The Rock" (Jn. 1:42). It is a remarkable fact that before Jesus had given him this name, the names "Cephas" or "Petros" were unknown to the Greek-speaking world. This is already a sign that our Lord intended a special vocation for Simon Peter as a rock-foundation of unity and stability for the apostolic band. In fact, the name Cephas was also remarkable in a Hebrew context. As the Catholic apologist Karl Keating has pointed out:

> The startling thing was that in the Old Testament ... the word was never used as a proper name for a man. If one were to turn to a companion and say, "From now on, your name is Asparagus," people would wonder. Why Asparagus? What is the meaning of it? What does it signify? Indeed, why Peter for Simon the fisherman? Why give him as a name a word only used for God before this moment?

> The Jews would give other names taken from nature, such as Barach (which means lightning; Jos. 19:45), Deborah (bee; Gen. 35:8), Rachel (ewe; Gen. 29:16), but not Rock. In the New Testament, James and John were surnamed Boanerges, Sons of Thunder, by Christ (Mk. 3:17), but that was never regularly used in place of their original names. Simon's new name supplanted the old.[2]

Jewish readers of St. John's gospel would have well-understood what Jesus was trying to say by naming Simon as Cephas, the Rock. It was an allusion to Isaiah 51:1-2:

> Hearken to me, you who pursue deliverance, you that seek the Lord; look to the rock from which you were hewn, and to the quarry from which you were digged. Look to Abraham your father ... for when he was but one I called him, and I blessed him, and made him many.

Stephen Ray explains:

> Abraham was the pinnacle or fountainhead of the covenant peo-ple. Peter is given the ... designation of "rock" as "patriarch" of

---

[2] Karl Keating, *Catholicism and Fundamentalism* (San Francisco: Ignatius Press, 1988), 205-206.

the New Covenant [people]. As Abram's name was changed [to Abraham], so was Simon's, to show a change in status, and to point to him as the starting point and foundation of the Church.[3]

In short, our Lord Jesus Christ gave to Simon this novel and striking name which eventually supplanted his old name. He must have had an important purpose in doing so — and the Catholic understanding of our Lord's intention here is further clarified and confirmed in the three famous "Petrine texts" of the New Testament.

First of all, Jesus promised the apostolic primacy or leadership role to Peter at Caesarea Philippi after Peter declared that Jesus is the Son of God (Mt. 16:17-19):

> Blessed are you, Simon Bar-Jona! For flesh and blood has not revealed this to you, but my Father who is in heaven. And I tell you, you are Peter, and on this rock I will build my church, and the powers of death shall not prevail against it. I will give you the keys of the kingdom of heaven, and whatever you bind on earth shall be bound in heaven, and whatever you loose on earth shall be loosed in heaven.

Secondly, at the Last Supper, Jesus promised that Peter would have a special vocation in the fledgling Church: that of strengthening the faith of the apostolic band (Lk. 22:31-32):

> Simon, Simon, behold, Satan demanded to have you [plural; i.e., all the apostles], that he might sift you [plural] like wheat, but I have prayed for you [singular: i.e., Peter] that your faith may not fail; and when you have turned again, strengthen your brethren.

After His Resurrection, Jesus appeared to Simon Peter first among the Twelve (Lk. 24: 34; I Cor. 15:5); later, He fulfilled His promises to Peter by conferring upon him a primacy of leadership as chief shepherd of Christ's flock (Jn. 21:15-17):

---

[3] Ray, op. cit., 41.

When they had finished breakfast, Jesus said to Simon Peter, "Simon, son of John, do you love me more than these?" He said to him, "Yes, Lord; you know that I love you." He said to him, "Feed my lambs." A second time he said to him, "Simon, son of John, do you love me?" He said to him, "Yes, Lord; you know that I love you." He said to him, "Tend my sheep." He said to him the third time, "Simon, son of John, do you love me?" Peter was grieved because he said to him the third time, "Do you love me?" And he said to him, "Lord, you know everything; you know that I love you." Jesus said to him, "Feed my sheep."

After the Ascension, we see Peter exercise his leadership role in numerous ways, for example, conducting the election of a new apostle (Acts 1:15 ff), preaching the first evangelistic sermon on Pentecost (Acts 2), exercising disciplinary authority over sinful Christians (Acts 5 and 8), admitting the first Gentile converts to the Church (Acts 10 and 11), and speaking persuasively at the first apostolic council (Acts 15). Peter frequently spoke in the name of the whole apostolic band (Acts 3:15, 10:41), and St. Paul recognized the preeminence of Peter in the city of Jerusalem (Gal. 1:18). It is also worth noting that in the lists of the apostles given in the gospels, Peter is *always* named first, though he was not the first apostle to be called, nor do these lists rank the apostles according to the order in which they saw the risen Lord. Rather, Peter heads the list simply because he is "first" (Mt. 10:2-4), "protos," first and foremost.

Alternative Theories: "Liberal" scholarship

Needless to say, there have been many challenges to this Catholic reading of the scriptural evidence down through the ages. Here I must confine my discussion only to the most serious and enduring challenges, leaving the more eccentric theories for your own research.

Certainly one of the most popular theories — among so-called "liberal" scholars, at any rate — is the claim that the first of our "Petrine primacy" texts, Matthew 16:17-19, is nothing but a fabrication and interpolation by the early Church, or by St. Matthew himself, and does not represent the words spoken by the historical Jesus. Reasons given for this skepticism include:

> (a) that Christ's commendation of Peter does not occur in the accounts of the other two evangelists who report the conversation at Caesarea Philippi (see Mk. 8:27 ff, Lk. 9:20 ff);

> (b) that this silence is especially strange in Mark's gospel, since an ancient tradition holds that Mark's gospel is based on the preaching and teaching of Peter himself;

> (c) that the word "church" (ecclesia) occurs only one other time in the gospels on the lips of Jesus (Mt. 18:17), making it doubtful that Jesus Himself ever used the word — at least not before His resurrection; and

> (d) that if at this point in His ministry, Jesus had promised apostolic primacy to Peter, then it is inexplicable why the other disciples later squabbled over which one of them was to be the greatest in the kingdom (see Lk. 9:46).

For my part, I do not find these arguments very convincing. After all, none of the evangelists was trying to write an *exhaustive biographical account* of the words and deeds of Jesus. St. John even tells us, at the end of his gospel: "there are also many other things which Jesus did; were every one of them to be written, I suppose that the world itself could not contain all the books that would be written" (Jn. 21:25). Thus, it is not surprising that some of the important words and deeds of Jesus, appear in only one gospel account. Each gospel writer picked those things from the vast treasury of our Lord's words and deeds that he wanted to include in his account in order to emphasize specific points about Christ. For this reason, some of the parables of Jesus, and stories about Jesus, which emphasize his universal love (e.g. The Good Samaritan) occur only in the Gospel according to St. Luke. St. Matthew's gospel, on the other hand, which focuses attention on Christ as the Messiah and founder of the apostolic community of faith, is, not surprisingly, the only gospel that recalls for us that Christ occasionally called this community His "Church," and that He promised the primacy in the Church to Peter at Caesarea Philippi. In short, we do not need to doubt the historical veracity of Christ's recorded words and deeds just because they occur in only one gospel account, for it is of the very nature of this form of literature — a "gospel" or "good news" account — to be historically quite selective.

In particular, Mark's silence regarding the primacy of Peter need not worry us. Mark was not present at Caesarea Philippi, but Matthew, who *was* present, *did* record Christ's promise to Peter. Perhaps Peter was not accustomed to preaching things laudatory to himself, and therefore Mark did not pick up these words from his preaching. Perhaps Mark knew of Christ's promise to Peter, but did not record these words because they were not to Mark's purpose, given the particular truths about Jesus that Mark wanted to emphasize in his gospel. Or perhaps the frequent repetition throughout Mark's gospel of Simon's Christ-given name, "Petros" (The Rock), was felt to be sufficient to emphasize Peter's role in the early Church. Any of these explanations will suffice.

Finally, it should be noted that scholars have never found any reliable ancient manuscripts of St. Matthew's gospel in which verses 17-19 are missing from Chapter 16. The textual evidence therefore supports the authenticity of the passage.

Far from accepting that Matthew 16:17-19 is a later interpolation and fabrication, we can find considerable internal evidence for the value of this passage as historical reportage.

The Protestant New Testament scholar Gunther Bornkamm, for example, called our attention to the future tense which Jesus used at Caesarea Philippi. Jesus said, "On this rock I *will* build my Church," and "I *will* give you the keys." Traditional paintings which show Jesus conferring the keys on Peter at this point in the gospel story are therefore inaccurate, because Jesus is obviously referring to some *future* time when authority will be conferred upon Peter. Indeed, there would have been no reason to confer ruling authority to "bind and loose" on any of the apostles while Jesus their Master was still with them in the flesh. In St. Matthew's gospel, the Resurrection of Jesus is seen as the time when Christ assumes the fullness of His authority (exousia) as Lord of all, and delegates a portion of that authority to His apostles. This pattern occurs in St. John's Gospel, too. The future tense that Jesus used in Matthew 16, therefore, fits in well with the overall pattern of the gospel story.

The literary structure of this dialogue at Caesarea Philippi also speaks of its authenticity and gives us a clue to its interpretation. As Msgr. Peter Elliott explains in his essay "You are Peter" (CTS, 1970):

> Jesus is a rabbi, teaching his disciples using the *targum* method, the questions and answers of an old-fashioned catechism. For Matthew this *targum* method develops into a dramatic dialogue of challenge and response...

> These verses are the climax of Matthew's story of Christ's ministry. Jesus makes a dramatic self-revelation. Peter says, "You are the Christ, the Son of the Living God." Jesus candidly accepts this title, and then imposes secrecy on his dis-

ciples. This is Matthew's main point. But woven through the
text is an answer to another question — not only "who is
Jesus?," but "who is Peter?" Who is the rough fisherman sud-
denly inspired to recognize the Truth?

In fact, the very wording of Matthew 16:17-19 makes it
probable that these words derive from Jesus himself. For
example, in verse 17, Jesus calls Peter "Simon, Son of John,"
which was the Palestinian way of calling someone by their
full name. He also refers to God as "my Father" rather than
more formally as "our Father" or "the Father." This calls to
mind Christ's own characteristic, intimate way of referring to
God as "Abba."

The rest of the passage, verses 18-19, solves the mystery
for us of why Jesus named Simon "the Rock" from their very
first meeting. Peter is promised the power of the keys, and the
authority to bind and loose. Now the "keys" was a phrase
derived from the ancient Israelite court, and symbolic of the
office of master of the palace, the royal steward and chief
deputy of the king (I Kings 4:6, 16:9, 18:3, Is. 22:22, 36:3,
37:2, Rev. 1:18). The one who holds the "keys" obviously
possesses *supreme, delegated jurisdiction*. Stephen Ray
explains in detail:

> We learn from Revelation 3:7 that Jesus is "the holy one, the
> true one, who has the key of David, who opens and no one
> shall shut, who shuts and no one opens." These words are
> obviously based on Isaiah 22 ... The kings of the Davidic
> covenant were the proud possessors of the "Keys of David,"
> signifying unquestioned royal authority. Jesus possesses
> these keys as heir to David's throne. ... Each king has a king-
> dom, and each king has an "official over the house" ... this is
> the case with all the Eastern kingdoms. The keys are the sign
> of authority, and they belong exclusively to the king. Kings,
> however, would delegate the keys [literally worn over the

shoulder] to the stewards or viziers of their kingdom. Jesus ascended the throne of David and then, through his death and resurrection, expanded the covenant to *all* men, not just to the Jews. God gave him all authority in heaven and earth; he was now the king of the eternal kingdom of God. He was the proud possessor of the royal keys of God's kingdom. What did he do with the "keys of the kingdom?" He delegated the keys to Peter. *Simon the fisherman became Peter the royal steward.*[4]

The words "bind" and "loose" that Jesus used were common ancient Jewish legal terms for "forbid" and "permit" in the community of faith, including matters of the Divine Law and its interpretation. In verse 19, Peter's decisions of "binding" and "loosing" are even promised heavenly ratification.

Most importantly, Jesus makes a "play on words" in verse 18 which was possible in his own language, Aramaic, but not in Hebrew or Greek. In Aramaic the name Peter, and the word "rock" would both be "Kepha" (just as in French one could say "You are 'Pierre,' and on this 'pierre' I will build my church"). The "rock" of the Church is therefore to be Peter himself, with the ruling "keys," and authority to "bind" and "loose."

In short, the Catholic Church argues that *here we have an authentic promise from Jesus Christ to confer a ministry of apostolic primacy on Peter as His vicar or chief deputy in the community of faith.* Peter is given supreme authority both of jurisdiction (the keys) and heavenly-ratified teaching (binding and loosing) in the Church of our Savior.

Some scholars argue that the words of Jesus from this passage actually may have been spoken by Christ *after* the

---

[4] Ibid., 268-269.

Resurrection, and that Matthew inserted them into the Caesarea Philippi story for reasons of literary effect. Indeed, such an explanation would adequately explain all of the objections to the authenticity of this passage listed above (letters a-d). Whether Our Lord spoke these words before or after the Resurrection, however, would not significantly affect the *interpretation* of these words of Christ by the Church. The fact is that He spoke them, and that they imply a special leadership ministry for the apostle Peter.

I believe I have now said enough to counter the charge that Matthew 16:17-19 is an early church fabrication. But we have yet to consider a very different challenge to the Catholic reading of Peter's primacy: namely the view of most Evangelical and Eastern Orthodox scholars that, although Christ's words in Matthew 16 are authentic, they are misinterpreted by the Catholic Church.

Alternative Theories: Evangelical and Orthodox

The Protestant scholar Alan Richardson in *A Theological Word Book of the Bible* argues that the "word play" in Matthew 16:18 is not precise. Peter himself can hardly be the rock on which the Church is built, Richardson claims, because elsewhere in the New Testament, the rock of the Church is said to be Christ Himself, or faith in Christ (I Cor. 3:11; 10:4; Heb. 11:10). Moreover, the Greek text contrasts the proper name for Peter, "Petros," meaning "stone fragment," with "petra," which means "rock."[5]

Once again, I do not find these arguments very convincing. Matthew hardly could have used the Greek word "petra," a *feminine* word, as a proper name for a *male*! This surely accounts for the slight variation in Greek between Peter

---

[5] Alan Richardson, *A Theological Word Book of the Bible* (New York: Macmillan, 1950), 204.

("Petros") and rock ("petra") in verse 18. We need to remember that Matthew was trying to translate into Greek a "word play" from Aramaic, the language Jesus spoke, in which the two words (Kepha) would have been identical. Matthew was therefore able to use "petra" for "rock," but for the proper name "Rock," for a male, he had to use "Petros" instead.

Furthermore, Matthew could have used the imagery of rock or stone in a different way than other New Testament writers: supplementing them without necessarily contradicting them. *Thus Peter can be seen as the Church's "rock," in so far as his ministry was built upon Christ, who is the ultimate foundation stone of the Church. There is no real contradiction here.* In other places in the New Testament, the foundation of the church is said to be the apostles and prophets (Eph. 2:20); or again, in Jesus' parable about building one's house upon the solid rock, the rock he refers to is the hearing and obeying of His own teachings (Mt. 7:24). The various New Testament uses of the metaphors of "rock" and "foundation" do not contradict each other in the least. In fact, all of the metaphors used in the New Testament to describe Peter's ministry are used in various ways in the Scriptures. Jesus is said to have the key to heaven (Rev. 3:7), but the keys to the kingdom are also delegated on earth, in another sense, to Peter. Jesus is the Good Shepherd, but Peter is also given the responsibility of being a special shepherd under the Good Shepherd, a responsibility given to him by the Good Shepherd Himself (Jn. 21:15-17); in another sense, every one of the Church's pastors is called to be a shepherd of the flock committed to his charge, under the chief shepherd, Jesus Christ (I Pt. 5:1-4). As the Protestant scholar George Salmon once wrote:

> It is undoubtedly the doctrine of Scripture that Christ is the only foundation: "other foundation can no man lay than that

is laid, which is Jesus Christ" (I Cor. 3:11). Yet we must remember that the same metaphor may be used to illustrate different truths, and so, according to circumstances, may have different significations. ... You see then that the fact that Christ is called the rock and that on Him the Church is built is no hindrance to Peter's also being, in a different sense, called rock, and said to be the foundation of the Church; so that I consider there is no ground for the fear entertained by some, in ancient and in modern times, that by applying the words personally to Peter, we should infringe on the honour due to Christ alone.[6]

While it is true that Christ reaffirms the name of "Rock" for Simon in *response* to his confession of faith in verse 16 ("You are the Christ, the Son of the living God"), it is also clear that *Peter* is to be the church's Rock, and not just his faith. Again, this is clear because in Aramaic, the language Jesus spoke, the two names "Peter" and "Rock" would have been identical. It is also clear because in later years, Simon's proper name drops out of use altogether, and he becomes known simply as Petros or Cephas, "Rock." The Rock is a *person* fulfilling a communal role, not just a confession of faith.

If we accept the Catholic interpretation of Matthew, Chapter 16, then we find it generally concurs with Luke 22:32. Here Jesus remarks at the Last Supper that He has prayed for Peter that his faith may not fail, and that he will turn again (future tense) and strengthen his brethren, namely after the Resurrection. Again, Peter's faith is certainly involved, but it is Peter, the person and minister of faith, who is to strengthen the apostolic church.

After the Resurrection, in John 21:15-17, Peter is given his special commission in a dramatic, threefold way, a way that also absolves him of his triple denial of his Master on the

---

[6] Ray, op. cit., 16.

night of Jesus' arrest. It is important to bear in mind that the Church was often called a "flock" by the early Christians (Acts 20:28; I Pt. 5:2), and in Biblical times, *the imagery of a shepherd, feeding and tending his flock, carries with it connotations not only of tender care, but also of authority* (see 2 Sam. 5:2; Is. 40:11; Ps. 77:20; 78:70-72; I Peter 5:2). For example, King David is called in the Psalms "the shepherd of Jacob his people, of Israel his inheritance. With upright heart he tended them, and guided them with a skillful hand" (Ps. 78:70-72). The elders of Israel at Hebron said to David: "It was you that led out and brought in Israel: and the Lord said to you. 'You shall be shepherd of my people Israel, and you shall be prince over Israel'" (2 Sam. 5:2). A shepherd has authority over his sheep, and so to feed and care for a flock of sheep implies the authority to rule as well as the duty to love.

Eastern Orthodox apologists sometimes claim that here in John 21, Peter is merely restored to his shepherding role as an *apostle*, equal to the other apostles, a role which he had lost through his triple denial of Christ. But if this is merely a restoration scene, why single out Peter for restoration? Except for the apostle John, all of the other apostles had abandoned Jesus and fled on that fateful night in the Garden of Gethsemane. Perhaps Peter alone was singled out because of his dramatic, threefold denial of Christ, in contrast with his proud boasting that he would *never* abandon Christ, even if all the other apostles did (Mt. 26:31 ff). The risen Jesus therefore asked him: "do you love me more than *these*?" — namely, *more than the other apostles*. By rights, Peter should have said "No Lord, John clearly loves You the most, since he stayed with You at the foot of the cross, while I denied You three times, despite boasting that I would be the last one to abandon You." But notice what Peter says instead. He says, with great hesitation, "Yes, Lord, you know that I love You," a kind of half-affirmative response to Jesus' question. Now, Our Lord could read hearts; He knew that Peter was neither lying, nor boasting this time. He was penitent and sincere. In fact, the risen Jesus had *already* forgiven Peter, and all the apostles, for the part they played in His passion. But he who is forgiven much, loves much (Lk. 7:41-47). Peter's special love for Christ was now proven not by proud boasting, but by the depth and sincerity of his repentance and his trust in the merciful love of his Savior. On this basis, Peter could truly give a hesitant "Yes, Lord," to Christ's question about loving Him "more than these," and Christ could therefore proceed with His plan to confer upon Peter a special responsibility to be universal shepherd of the fledgling church. How different the history of the Church might have been if the successors of Peter had always borne this in mind: if they had always remembered that their office was built not only upon Christ's promises after Peter's confession of faith at Caesarea Philippi, but also upon Christ's *forgiveness* and Peter's *penitence!*

Nevertheless, some commentators suggest that in John 21, Christ's call to Peter to "feed my sheep" simply means that he was to do what all the other apostles were to do: feed the various flocks which would be committed to their charge. But notice: Jesus does not say "feed *your* sheep but "feed *my* sheep." Christ is the Chief Shepherd, according to the New Testament, and *all Christians together, including the apostles, are Christ's flock, His sheep* (Heb. 13:20); hence, by saying "feed *my* sheep" to Peter, Jesus meant "rule and tend and care for *my whole flock*, including your brother apostles" (in this way Peter was to do what Christ had prayed he would do in Luke 22:32 — "strengthen your brethren"). *This is Peter's special commission — "feed my sheep," rule and care for the whole universal Church.* Thus, just as the rabbis of ancient

Israel often used a ritual formula that was repeated three times in the act of solemnly transferring authority in the Jewish community of faith, in a similar way, Jesus bestowed authority on Peter to be the chief and universal shepherd of His sheep, repeating three times His call: "feed my sheep."

St. John Chrysostom summed up the issue in his 88th homily on John's Gospel:

> And why, having passed by the others, doth He speak with Peter on these matters? He was the chosen one of the apostles, the mouth of the disciples, the leader of the band; on this account also, Paul went upon a time to inquire of him rather than the others. ... He [our Lord] putteth into his hands the rule over the brethren.

Evangelical and Orthodox scholars, who reject the Catholic interpretation of the three great "Petrine texts," often argue that these three texts need to be interpreted in the light of the New Testament as a whole. In that wider context, we see that *Peter did not exercise a monarchical role among the apostles.* For example, Christ extended the authority to "bind and loose" to all the apostles in Matthew 18:18, and in Ephesians 2:20, the whole apostolic band, along with the prophets, is said to be the "foundation" upon which the Church is built. All the apostles together decided upon the disputed question of the mission to the Gentiles in Acts 15:23-25. In one place in Scripture, Peter and John are even said to be "sent" by the apostles to Samaria (Acts 8:14) — a strange thing for a monarch to be "sent" somewhere by his court! It is arguable that Peter deferred to the authority of James, the cousin of the Lord, at the Jerusalem Council (Acts 15:18). In fact, we read in Scripture that Paul once rebuked Peter to his face (Gal. 2:11) and Paul mentions James and John as "pillars" of the ancient Church along with Peter (Gal.

2:9). In short, Peter certainly does not seem to act as "Sovereign Pontiff" of the apostolic Church!

Once again, however, I do not think this line of argument stands up under close scrutiny.

Doubtless, Peter did not realize or exercise the *fullness* of his special apostolic ministry in the New Testament era, because the full implications of Christ's special commission to Peter naturally would take time to clarify and appreciate. After all, as we have seen, the words "rock" and "keys" which Jesus had used, and the concept of "shepherd," were filled with meaning, and all this would naturally take time for the Church community to unfold, drawing out its implications under the guidance of the Holy Spirit. In this respect, the doctrine of the Petrine Ministry is no different from the Christian doctrine of the Incarnation and the Holy Trinity: doctrines rooted in the words and deeds of Jesus, yet taking centuries to elucidate and clarify in the early Church.

Nevertheless, as we have already seen, a number of passages in the New Testament do seem to support the Catholic view that the early Church recognized in Peter a special Christ-given leadership role in the community of faith. With regard to those passages which seem to imply something less than pre-eminent authority for Peter, we can reply as follows:

(a) The fact that Peter, James, and John were described together as "pillars" by St. Paul in Galatians 2:9, does not contradict the pre-eminence that Paul seems to accord to Peter elsewhere in that same epistle (see Gal. 1:18). Besides, Peter is not called Simon in 2:9, but Cephas, "Rock," implying a special pre-eminent role for Peter amongst these three "pillars." Similarly, as we shall see, the recognition of five leading patriarchates in the ancient Christian world (Rome, Alexandria, Antioch, Jerusalem and Constantinople) did not contradict the fact that one of them (Rome) was generally accorded "pre-eminent authority" by the early Christian community.

(b) It is not true that James presided over the first apostolic council in Jerusalem. In fact, it was Peter who spoke decisively on the doctrinal issue in question at that council, for as Acts 15:12 tells us, after Peter finished speaking "all the assembly kept silence." His words sealed the unity of the assembly. St. James only added scriptural support and practical applications to what St. Peter had already stated. In any case, it was not necessary for anyone to "pull rank" on anyone else at this council, because the persuasive words of Peter and Paul were more than enough to form a common mind among the apostles and elders on this occasion.

(c) The fact that Peter allowed himself to be "sent" with John to Samaria may only mean that he was wise enough and humble enough to recognize the guidance of the Holy Spirit in the consensus of the apostles asking them to go. Similarly, popes down through the ages have often responded favourably to petitions from the college of bishops, for example, when Pope Pius IX was flooded with requests to proclaim the doctrine of the Immaculate Conception; or when Pope John Paul II acceded to the request of the Synod of Bishops to write an encyclical on Christian ethics. He actually went the "extra mile" for them, and wrote *two* such encyclicals!

(d) The fact that Paul rebuked Peter to his face in Galatians 2:11 only implies that Peter, though pre-eminent pastor of the Church, was still a sinful, and in most respects fallible human being — afflictions shared by every subsequent pope. Indeed, great saints have often rebuked popes. In the 14th century, for example, St. Catherine of Siena rebuked a pope for failing to return the papal residence from Avignon to Rome. In the 16th century, St. Philip Neri sent a letter to the Pope admonishing him for his conduct. In short, there is nothing about the Catholic doctrine of the Petrine Ministry that implies that the bearer of this office in the Church always will be virtuous and upright in character. From Peter himself, down to the present day, those carrying on his role and ministry have sometimes fallen into sin and hypocrisy, and sometimes have needed correction.

(e) Finally, the Catholic Church does not deny that it is implicit in the New Testament that in some sense all the apostles, together with Peter, were foundation stones of the Church, and that all were to be shepherds with Peter, and to help govern the Church by "binding" and "loosing" (Eph. 2:20, I Pt. 5:2, Mt. 18:18). Catholics simply point to two remarkable scriptural facts: 1). that Peter alone was given the "keys" as Christ's chief deputy, and called to shepherd Christ's whole flock; and 2). that *all the authority for ministry promised to the apostles collectively (Peter included) was initially and explicitly promised to Peter alone by Jesus Christ*. What all the apostles are together as a group, therefore, Peter sums up in his own ministry:

> You are Peter, and on this rock I will build my church, and the powers of death shall not prevail against it. I will give you the keys of the kingdom of heaven ... to bind ... and to loose ... strengthen your brethren ... feed my sheep.

The Petrine Ministry

All things considered, it seems clear that the early Church preserved a memory that the apostle Peter was called to a special leadership ministry by the Lord Jesus. While

Peter shares in the authority for ministry given to the whole apostolic band, *to Peter alone was given the ministry of being the rock of the Church, chief key-bearing deputy of the heavenly King, strength of the apostolic band, and shepherd of the universal church.* Of course, this does not mean that Peter was called to be a mere institutional official. On the contrary, as John 21:18-19 makes clear, the nature of Peter's call to be first shepherd under the Good Shepherd includes the readiness to become a suffering servant of the Lord, identifying with the Cross of Christ. In this respect, John 21 echoes Christ's view of His own ministry, and of Christian ministry in general (Mk. 10:43-45, RSV):

> Whoever would be greatest among you must be your servant, and whoever would be first among you must be slave of all. For the Son of Man also came not to be served but to serve, and to give his life as a ransom for many.

I am reminded at this point of the favourite title of Pope St. Gregory the Great for his own papal ministry: "Servus Servorum Dei" — Servant of the Servants of God.

Peter's special vocation and responsibility certainly did not insure that he would be perfect, or free from error in every respect. In fact, his call to be rock and universal shepherd of the Church stands in sharp contrast to the many times in the New Testament we see Peter fall, or misunderstand Jesus, or fail in courage. For example, Peter sinks in the waves on the Sea of Galilee (Mt. 14:30); he alone is rebuked by Jesus, "Get behind me, Satan" for his blindness to Christ's true Messianic role (Mt. 16:22). Peter denies Jesus three times on the night of his Master's arrest (Mt. 26:69 ff), and he is also the only apostle whom we see rebuked by Paul (Gal. 2:11). In other words, despite his special call to leadership, the New Testament shows quite clearly that true sanctity was something that Peter attained only gradually, and with great difficulty. His place of leadership, therefore, cannot be explained by any initial or supreme possession of qualities such as courage or wisdom. His leadership role rested on Christ's promise and grace, and not on Peter's virtues. In short, when Jesus named Simon "the Rock," it was not meant as a *description* of Peter, but as a *calling*. Peter grew in stature only gradually, with the help of divine grace, as he sought to fulfill the vocation which he had been given by the risen Lord.

Finally, among the three "pillars" of the apostolic Church — Peter, James and John — Peter's special leadership role among the apostles was the only role that conceivably could be passed down to later generations. No successor of James could claim to be another cousin of the Lord, nor receive another special resurrection appearance, such as James had received (I Cor. 15:7). No successor of John could be the disciple whom Jesus most intimately loved (Jn. 13:23). The basis of their special leadership roles in the community died with them. But Peter was given the ministerial role of rock, chief deputy, strength, and universal shepherd. Surely, the Church would always need a rock of unity and stability; her apostolic bishops and pastors would always need to be strengthened in faith; the heavenly King would always need a chief deputy on earth; and the flock as a whole would always need to be fed with the truth of Christ.

Before we leave this discussion of the scriptural evidence, we shall have to consider the question: should there be — indeed, *can* there be — *successors* to Peter's ministry in the life of the Church? And what light, if any, does the New Testament shed for us on this question?

Petrine Succession

Catholics argue that some form of social, organic unity in the Church is clearly called for in Ephesians 1:9-10, and 4:11-13, where St. Paul writes:

> For he has made known to us in all wisdom and insight the mystery of his will, according to his purpose which he set forth in Christ as a plan for the fullness of time, *to unite all things in him*, things in heaven and things on earth. ... and his gifts were that some should be apostles, some prophets, some evangelists, some pastors and teachers to equip the saints for the work of ministry, *for building up the body of Christ, until we all attain to the unity of the faith ... .*

There is, then, one Body of Christ, through which and in which all things are to be united in Christ's grace, truth, and love, through the working of the various ministries of the one Body. It is this fullness of unity in the Church, both visible and invisible, for which our Lord had prayed on the eve of His passion: "that they all may be one, as thou Father, in me, and I in thee, that they also may be one in us: that the world may believe that thou has sent me..." (Jn. 17:21).

Given New Testament passages such as these, we should expect that Jesus would have provided His Church with a continuing particular ministry (or ministries) whose first responsibility would be to *keep* the universal Church in that state of unity for which Christ had prayed, and which was to be so painstakingly built up by the work of all: by apostles, prophets, evangelists, pastors, teachers, and so on.

That unifying ministry, first of all, was the *apostolic ministry*, for we see the fledgling Church united in the apostles teaching and fellowship, the breaking of bread and the prayers in communion with the apostles (Acts 2:42).

Moreover, when disputes arose in the universal Church, it was the council of the apostles, together with the elders, that passed judgment on such matters (Acts 15). In the Catholic tradition, therefore, it is those who are called to carry on this apostolic-leadership ministry, the college of bishops, upon whom responsibility chiefly rests for preserving the unity of the universal Church in truth and love.

But of course, Catholics believe there is "more to the story" than that.

In several places, scripture speaks of Jesus Christ Himself as "head" of the Church, the one who builds up and preserves the unity of His Body (Eph. 4:15). He does this principally through the leadership, preaching, and teaching of the apostolic ministry ("He that receives you, receives Me" — Mt. 10:40) and through His Holy Eucharist, by which Christ makes us "one bread, one body" in Him (I Cor. 10:17). In a few places, however, scripture identifies Christ not just with the "head," but with the whole body of the Church (I Cor. 12:12, 27; and implicitly in Jn. 15:4-5). St. Paul teaches that the Spirit of Christ Jesus animates and vivifies the whole universal body, uniting and harmonizing the work of its members and organs, much as the human soul informs, vivifies, and directs a human body (see I Cor. 12:4-31). This makes it probable that there will be an earthly, visible "head" in Christ's universal Body, just as in St. Paul's analogy there are other visible "members" and organs in the Body, "eyes," "hands," "feet," and so on, differing in function and office. The Eastern Orthodox theologian Nicholas Afanassief recognized the force of this scriptural analogy when he wrote:

> We cannot refute the doctrine of universal primacy by saying that the Church has Christ as Head; that is an indisputable truth and the supporters of primacy do not themselves oppose it. The real question is: if the Church has an invisible Head

(Christ) can she, or can she not, also have a visible head? If not, then why can a local church have a single head in the person of the bishop? In other words, why can one part of the Universal Church have a single (visible) head, while the entire Universal Church is deprived of one?[7]

Still, one might wish to argue that this universal, visible headship-ministry need not reside in an individual. Theoretically, it could reside instead in synods, and ecumenical councils of bishops and church leaders.

Needless to say, the Catholic Church argues that *it was the express will of Jesus Christ to establish a special, unifying, leadership or "headship" ministry in the person of Peter, and his successors.*

First of all, why would our Lord have promised to Peter a special vocation and leadership role among the apostles as the rock of the Church, and as key-bearing chief deputy of the heavenly King, and in nearly the same breath say that the "powers of death" would not prevail against the Church, if death was indeed to be the end of the very vocation within the Church which Jesus had just promised to establish (Mt. 16:18)? The phrase Jesus used, "the powers of death shall not prevail against it," *occurs in the very midst of His promises to Peter*, "sandwiched" in between them, as it were. This implies that our Lord was looking to what was good for His Church in the long run, transcending the gates of death, the passing away of successive generations. Implicit in our Lord's words, therefore, is a long-term Petrine Primacy.

Secondly, the role of key-bearer (royal steward, chief deputy of the King) which Jesus had given to Peter implies succession, when understood in the light of Scripture as a whole. Stephen Ray summarizes for us the Biblical evidence:

---

[7] John Meyendorff, ed., *The Primacy of Peter in the Orthodox Church* (Crestwood, N.Y.: St. Vladimir's Seminary Press, 1992), 18.

During the reign of Solomon, we first discover Ahishar, who is "over the house" in 1 Kings 4:6. Ahishar seems to be the first person recorded in the Bible to be delegated with the keys of David, though he is not necessarily the first royal steward. Next we find Arza as steward "over the house" during the reign of King Elah (I Kings 16:9). The next recorded steward is Obadiah, who was "over the house" during the reign of King Ahab (I Kings 18:3). About 150 years later, Isaiah prophecies against Shebna and foretells the appointment of his successor, Eliakim (Is 22:22). The Scriptures show us that the office of steward was one of succession — it was always filled. The keys of David were passed from one steward to the next throughout the history of Israel and later also in Judah.[8]

In any case, it would be odd indeed to claim that Peter's special vocation in the apostolic Church was completely personal to him, and that once he had died, that ministry came to an end. As Fr. Roderick Strange stated in his book *The Catholic Faith*, Roman Catholics

> accept that there was something personal about Peter's ministry which makes it indeed irreplaceable and unique, but they go on to argue that it cannot have been a ministry locked into its own time altogether. Christian generations do not exist as self-contained islands. It is the same Church, whether we are talking about the first century, or the twentieth. Its essential character and activities persist. Peter's ministry is as much a part of its life now as it was and has always been. ... throughout history the Church will need *its rock; it will need to be strengthened and it will need to be fed.*[9]

Of course, in one sense, apostles cannot have "successors." The original band of apostles were foundation stones for the Church in a unique and unrepeatable sense: as the original, chosen witnesses of the saving work of Jesus Christ.

---

[8] Ray, op. cit., 291.
[9] Roderick Strange, *The Catholic Faith* (Oxford: Oxford University Press, 1986).

Nevertheless, important aspects of the commission they received from Christ could not possibly have been completed by them in their lifetime (such as the charge to "Go and make disciples of *all* nations ... ." Mt. 28:20). According to the earliest Church Fathers such as St. Clement and St. Ireneus, the apostolic leadership role was passed on to delegated successors in the early Church, to carry on that leadership ministry and to fulfill that commission (cf. Acts 14:23, 2 Tim. 1:6, Titus 1:5). Similarly, it seems clear from Scripture that a *Petrine Ministry — in other words, a ministry of personal, visible headship in Christ's Body, to serve and secure the Church's unity in truth and love —* is Jesus Christ's will for the continuing life of His Church, just as it was His will for the first generation of Christians.

II. The Petrine Ministry in the Patristic Era

In our first chapter, I sought to provide you with a Catholic perspective on the Petrine texts in Scripture, as well as on the role of Peter more generally in the New Testament. I finished by touching upon the New Testament seeds of the notion of Petrine succession, in the context of St. Paul's understanding of the Church as the universal Body of Christ.

This way of understanding the Church, and the role of the Petrine Ministry within the Church, received classic expression in the great encyclical "Mystici Corporis" of Pope Pius XII in 1943. In this document, the Pope pondered the many ways in which the Church can be said to be the Mystical Body of Christ. He tells us, first of all, that the Church is a *social Body*: one, undivided, visible, constituted organically and hierarchically, endowed with vital means of grace (especially the Sacraments); it is composed of individual members, including sinners. Secondly, the Pope says, the Church is the Body of *Christ*; Christ was its founder: by preaching, by suffering and dying for us on the Cross, and by pouring out His Spirit upon us at Pentecost. Christ today, as invisible "Head" of His Body, enlightens, sanctifies, and saves the Church: in invisible (and sometimes extraordinary) ways, but also in a visible and ordinary way, guiding and governing His Body through the ministry of the bishop in each local and particular Church, and through the Roman Pontiff in the universal Church. Finally, Pope Pius XII teaches that the Church is the *Mystical* Body of Christ, in that "the Spirit of our Redeemer... penetrates and fills every part of the

Church's being and is active within it until the end of time, as the source of every grace and every gift and every miraculous power" (par. 63).

In this overall picture of the Church as the universal, Mystical Body of Christ, the Petrine Primacy plays a vital role. The Primacy is the visible head of the Body (par. 40):

> You know, venerable Brethren, that after He had ruled the "little flock" Himself during His mortal pilgrimage, Christ our Lord, when about to leave this world and return to the Father, entrusted to the Chief of the Apostles the visible government of the entire community He had founded. Since He was all wise He could not leave the Body of the Church He had founded as a human society without a visible head. Nor against this may one argue that the primacy of jurisdiction established in the Church gives such a Mystical Body two heads. For Peter in virtue of his primacy is only Christ's Vicar; so that there is only one chief Head of this Body, namely Christ, who never ceases to guide the Church invisibly, though at the same time He rules it visibly, through him who is His representative on earth. After His glorious Ascension into Heaven this Church rested not on Him alone, but on Peter too, its visible foundation stone. That Christ and His Vicar constitute one only Head is the solemn teaching of our predecessor of immortal memory Boniface VIII in the Apostolic Letter "Unam Sanctam"; and his successors have never ceased to repeat the same.

In short, our risen Lord exercises His Headship over His Mystical Body visibly — though not exclusively — in and through His Vicar on earth, the successor of St. Peter.

Suffice it to say that the argument I am presenting to you is the clear teaching of the papal Magisterium down through the ages. I have argued that in the New Testament, Jesus the Saviour explicitly promised, and later bestowed upon the apostle Peter, a special leadership ministry described as rock of the Church, chief deputy of the heavenly King, strengthener of the apostolic band, and universal shepherd of the sheep; I have also argued that it is implicit in our Lord's words, and in the New Testament understanding of the Church more generally, that the Petrine Ministry was not to be "locked into" its own time altogether, but was to be a continuous feature of the life of the Church. Moreover, the Petrine Ministry fulfills the role of visible "head" of the universal Church Body, in and through which her invisible Head, Jesus Christ, principally guides and governs His Body, building up and preserving her unity in truth and love. For this reason also the pope is truly called "the Vicar of Christ": as the chief instrument, representative, and expression of the headship of the risen Lord, Jesus Christ, in and over His universal, Mystical Body. Through the Petrine Ministry, therefore, out of His infinite love for us, Our Saviour shepherds, guides and unifies His flock.

Other New Testament Models of the Church

Needless to say, one would be quite wrong to pretend that this image of the Church as the universal Body of Christ is the *only* way to understand the Church presented in the New Testament. Scripture also teaches, for example, that the Church is the pilgrim People of God and the mystical Bride of Christ. I have concentrated on the "Body of Christ" simply because I believe that is the most prominent conception of the Church to be found in the New Testament. Nothing about the other "images" of the Church in Scripture, however, contradicts Catholic teaching regarding the papacy (eg., the pilgrim People of God need a visible, principal Shepherd for their journey, just as the People of Israel were given Moses, and later Joshua for their shepherds on their journey to the Promised Land).

Before moving on, however, I want to comment upon two other scriptural "lenses" through which we can view the Church: first the Church as an icon of the Holy Trinity, and second the Church as a "koinonia" (communion-fellowship) of local churches. Both of these lenses are helpful to us in understanding aspects of the mystery of the Church, but neither one, I would argue, contradicts the primacy of the Petrine Ministry.

(1) In his popular book *The Orthodox Church*, Bishop Kallistos Ware tells us that the phrase "image of the Holy Trinity" is vital to the Eastern Orthodox understanding of the Church:

> The Church as a whole is an icon of God the Trinity, reproducing on earth the mystery of the unity in diversity. In the Trinity the three are one God, yet each is fully personal; in the Church a multitude of human persons are united in one, yet each preserves his personal diversity unimpaired ... .

> This conception of the Church as an icon of the Trinity has many further applications. Unity in diversity — just as each person of the Trinity is autonomous, so the Church is made up of a number of independent Autocephalous Churches; and just as in the Trinity the three persons are equal, so in the Church no one bishop can claim to wield an absolute power over all the rest.

> This idea of the Church as an icon of the Trinity also helps us to understand the Orthodox emphasis upon Councils. A council is an expression of the Trinitarian nature of the Church. The mystery of unity in diversity according to the image of the Trinity can be seen in action, as the many bishops assembled in council freely reach a common mind under the guidance of the Spirit.[10]

Bishop Ware also might have pointed to the scriptural roots of this perspective on the Church: our Lord praying

[10] Timothy Ware, *The Orthodox Church* (Middlesex: Penguin Books, 1980), 244-245.

before His Passion "that they all may be one, as we (the Father and the Son) also are one" (Jn. 17:22). In any case, it is a beautiful image of the Church, and, one might say "true as far as it goes."

However, I do not think it strikes any blow against the universal, Petrine Primacy. Quite the contrary. The doctrine of the Trinity, insofar as it is common to both East and West, teaches that the divine Trinity consists of three co-equal, co-eternal persons in one divine nature. However, there is also one ultimate source (or "arche") of the unity of the three, the eternal Father, from whom the other two persons eternally come to be. The eternal, ultimate source of the Trinity is therefore the overflowing love of the Father; there is a "primacy," if you will, in the eternal Trinity itself: not a primacy of nature but of *origin*. On this analogy there ought to be an office of "Holy Fatherhood" in the universal Church, just as there is a primacy of "Holy Fatherhood" in the eternal life of the Trinity.

Of course, this image cannot be pressed too far: the Roman Pontiff, as supreme "Holy Father" in the Church, is not the sole or ultimate source of the whole life of the Church. For example, he is not the source of baptismal grace in the Church, nor of the gifts of the Spirit. In fact, the Petrine Ministry is only one of many sources of divine life and action in the Church, for the Pope is but the principal "episcope" (overseer) of the divine life of Christ's Body, our universal shepherd and rock of unity.

The idea of the Church as "image of the Trinity" also breaks down because it is too idealistic. Of course the Church would be a perfect image of the Trinity if we were all perfected saints, united in spontaneous love and truth. But we are not. We are all sinners, not yet fully cured. Hence, autocephalous churches frequently fall out of communion with one another over ethnic and jurisdictional disputes. Bishops all too frequently remain divided among themselves over matters of doctrine and discipline, even when they meet together in ecumenical council. Such is the lesson of history. And that is one reason why the universal Church cannot always rely for its governance on autonomous bishops and autocephalous churches freely and spontaneously cooperating with one another. The Holy Spirit ever works to effect such cooperation as much as possible. But the Holy Spirit also works in the universal Church to rescue it from sin and division, and to secure its unity, especially through the authority of the See of St. Peter, the chief deputy of Christ and the visible head of the one Body. In fact, the Petrine Ministry is first of all the representative, icon and Vicar of Christ, *our Savior from sin,* the Bridegroom of His Bride, the Shepherd of His flock. The papacy is only indirectly an image of the Father who sent Him.

In a sense, then, the Church is meant to be a living icon of the Holy Trinity, but like all images, this image has its limitations; it needs to be balanced by other scriptural models, and the model supports rather than contradicts the need for a universal pastor and primate, a unifying "Holy Father."

(2) The universal Church is sometimes said to be a "koinonia" or communion-fellowship of local churches. This doctrine is very prominent in ecumenical documents of the Church, not the least in Catholic-Orthodox dialogue statements. Scripture sometimes speaks of each local church as fully "the Church" (e.g. I Cor. 1:2, Rev. 1:20). Indeed, each Holy Eucharist is the Eucharist of the whole church; we never partake of a "part" of Christ at Holy Communion, nor is the local eucharistic celebration merely a "part" of some

larger Eucharist. Rather, each local Eucharist is a full manifestation of the Church in each place it is celebrated, a micro-
cosm, if you will, of the whole, universal Body. The universal Church can therefore be seen as a communion of local
churches in faith and charity: a communion of communions,
one might say.

Once again, there is nothing here that necessarily vio-
lates Catholic teaching about the universal Petrine Ministry.
Quite the contrary. On this view, the local Church manifests
the plenitude of the Church — yet it can hardly do so in iso-
lation; it can only do so in the measure of its communion
with all the other Churches. Authentic local churches, therefore, are bonded together with other local churches by a common faith and "communio in sacris" (sacramental communion). But how is this common faith to be defined and
secured? And how are these bonds of communion to be maintained when disputes arise? Does the history of the Church
show that synods and councils of bishops *alone* can maintain
these bonds? Does not the New Testament show that as a gift
of His love, Jesus Christ has provided His Mystical Body
with another instrument of unity as well: *the Petrine Ministry, as rock and universal shepherd of the Church?* Does
not the worldwide Church need a universal shepherd to
secure the communion of the local churches in truth and love;
*a primate with sufficient authority, as chief apostle, and
Vicar of Christ, to intervene in any local church or region of
churches, wherever the fullness of faith, or proper bonds of
communion among the churches, are in jeopardy?* Even so,
the First Vatican Council teaches in its preamble to the "First
Dogmatic Constitution on the Church of Christ" (1870):

> In order that the episcopate also might be one and undivided,
> and that by means of a closely united priesthood the multi-

tude of the faithful might be kept secure in the oneness of faith and communion, He (our Lord) set Blessed Peter over the rest of the Apostles, and fixed in him the abiding principle of this twofold unity and its visible foundation, in the strength of which the everlasting temple should arise, and the Church in the firmness of that faith should lift her majestic front to heaven.

Nevertheless, Eastern writers insist that it is Christ Jesus Himself, the divine Word made flesh, who ensures the unity of His mystical Body through the Eucharistic gift of Himself. Where the Eucharist is celebrated, and Christians are united in Him, the *totality* of the mystery of the Church is made present. Any other principle of unity or universality it is claimed, is inessential. The unity of Christ's Church, therefore, does not call for a Petrine "superstructure" as its institutional guarantee.

However, in its 1992 document entitled, *Some Aspects of the Church Understood as Communion,* the Congregation for the Doctrine of the Faith (CDF) pointed out that it is precisely the "one bread ... one body" of the Lord, given and received in each Eucharist, that calls for visible expression and fulfillment in the one, unified, universal Body of the Lord. That is why the Eucharist in each parish or particular Church must be celebrated in union and communion with the local bishop who is the guarantee of the unity of the presbyterate in each diocese; according to ancient tradition, the local bishop himself must be consecrated by at least three bishops from other local Churches (i.e., the local Church cannot create its own bishop for its own local Eucharist), and the bishop of each local Church must maintain proper bonds of communion with all of the other local Churches and their bishops, in the unity of the one faith, and the one episcopate (in the early Church, this was maintained by the necessity of remaining in communion with the principal Sees, especially Rome, Alexandria and Antioch Sees which provided not a "superstructure" but a "skeletal structure" for the unity of the universal Body). Each local Church — and its Eucharist — was thereby linked in a life-giving and life-receiving communion with all of the other local Churches. Hence, the CDF wrote:

> Indeed, the oneness and indivisibility of the eucharistic body of the Lord implies the oneness of his mystical body, which is the one and indivisible Church. *From the eucharistic center arises the necessary openness of every celebrating community, of every particular Church. By allowing itself to be drawn into the open arms of the Lord, it achieves insertion into his one and undivided body.* For this reason too, the existence of the Petrine ministry, which is the foundation of the unity of the episcopate and of the universal Church, bears a profound correspondence to the eucharistic character of the Church.... .

> The unity of the Eucharist and the unity of the episcopate *with Peter and under Peter* are not independent roots of the unity of the Church, since Christ instituted the Eucharist and the episcopate as essentially interlinked realities. The episcopate is one, just as the Eucharist is one: the one sacrifice of the one Christ, dead and risen. The liturgy expresses this reality in various ways, showing, for example, that every celebration of the Eucharist is performed in union not only with the proper bishop, but also with the Pope, with the episcopal order, with all the clergy, and with the entire people. Every valid celebration of the Eucharist expresses this universal communion with Peter and with the whole Church, or objectively calls for it, as in the case of the Christian churches separated from Rome.

In short, communion with Jesus Christ in the Eucharist in any local, or particular Church calls for communion with all those who are "in Christ" through the Eucharist; one cannot be fully united with Him without being fully in communion with His whole universal Body.

An in-depth examination of this issue from a Catholic perspective can be found in Cardinal Joseph Ratzinger's book, *Called to Communion* (Ignatius Press edition, 1996). Basing his discussion upon Scripture and ancient Patristic Tradition, Cardinal Ratzinger argues that the full Eucharistic reality of the local Church demands its participation in the universal communion of Churches:

> In the Eucharist I can never demand communion with Jesus alone. He has given Himself a [universal] Body. Whoever receives Him in Communion necessarily communicates with all His brothers and sisters who have become members of the one Body. *Communio includes the dimension of catholicity by virtue of the range of the mystery of Christ. ...*
>
> Orthodox theologians have contrasted the Eucharistic ecclesiology of the East, which they hold up as the authentic model of the Church, to the centralistic ecclesiology of Rome. In every local Church, they maintain, the whole mystery of the Church is present when the Eucharist is celebrated, because Christ is wholly present; there is thus nothing more to be added ... the idea of a Petrine office is contradictory; it resorts to a worldly pattern of unity that is opposed to the sacramental unity represented in the Church's Eucharistic constitution. Of course, this modern Orthodox Eucharistic ecclesiology is not defined in purely "local" terms, since the point from which it is constructed is the bishop, not the place as such. If one considers this fact, it becomes obvious that for the Orthodox tradition the mere celebration of the liturgical act in the given locality does not suffice to constitute the Church; a complementary principle is needed... .
>
> In the apostolic period it is above all the figure of the apostle itself that stands outside of the local principle. The apostle is not the bishop of a community but rather a missionary for the whole Church. The figure of the apostle is the strongest refutation of every purely local conception of the Church. He expresses in his person the universal Church; he

is her representative, and no local Church can claim him for herself alone. Paul carried out this function of unity by means of his letters and a network of messengers. These letters are an exercise of his catholic ministry of unity, which can be accounted for only by the apostle's authority in the Church universal... .

The Church cannot become a static juxtaposition of essentially self-sufficient local Churches. The Church must remain "apostolic," that is to say, the dynamism of unity must mold her structure. The epithet "successor of the apostles" removes the bishop beyond the purely local and makes it his responsibility to ensure that the two dimensions of *communio* — the vertical and horizontal — remain undivided ... membership in the communion, that is, membership in the Church, is by its essence universal. Whoever belongs to *one* local Church belongs to *all*. The consciousness, of this fact gave rise to the institution of letters of communion, which were termed *litterae communicatoriae, tesserae, symbola, litterae pacis* or the like, and which served to secure the unity of the *communio* and to draw clear boundaries over against the pretensions of false communions. Whenever a Christian went on a journey, he carried such a proof of membership; with it he would find lodging in every Christian community around the world and, as the center of this hospitality, communion in the Body of the Lord. ... In order for the system to function, the bishops for their part had to keep up-to-date lists of the more important Churches around the world with which they were in communion. "This list served as a register of addresses when it was necessary to issue the passes, and on the other side, the passes of arriving travelers were checked against this list."

Here we see a very concrete way in which the bishop is the ligature of catholicity. He keeps his Church connected with the others and thus embodies the apostolic and therefore, the catholic element of the Church. This fact is expressed in his very consecration: no community can simply give itself its own bishop. Such a radical embedding in the local is incompatible with the principle of apostolicity, and hence of universality. ... The bishop is consecrated by a group of at least three neighboring bishops, who also verify that he professes the same creed ... [A bishop] embodies the unity and the public character of the local Church that derive from the unity of Word and sacrament ... He is at the same time the link connecting his Church to the other local Churches: just as he answers for the unity of the Church in his territory, in his diocese, it is also incumbent upon him to mediate and constantly enliven the unity of his local Church with the entire, one Church of Jesus Christ. He must be solicitous for the catholic and apostolic dimensions of his local Church ...

The Council of Nicea, by its own declaration, was merely confirming ancient tradition when it laid down the primacies of Rome, Alexandria, and Antioch, and defined them as the hinges of the universal *communio*. The warrant of these three sees lies in the Petrine principle, as does the basis of Rome's apostolic responsibility to be the norm of unity. Consequently, both neighborly solicitude and living relation with Rome pertain to the catholicity of a bishop as ways of giving and receiving in the great communion of the one Church ... .[11]

The Petrine Primacy and the City of Rome

All this still leaves us with questions: if there is to be a Petrine leadership ministry, *where does it reside? Why the See of Rome?* There are some, for example, who have argued that since the tragic schism between East and West in the Middle Ages, a universal primacy of sorts passed to the Ecumenical Patriarchate in Constantinople, the "New Rome," or later, after the fall of Constantinople to the Muslims, to Moscow, "the Third Rome."

Catholics argue that the Petrine Ministry instituted by Jesus Christ resides in the See of Rome as a gift of divine providence, in other words, as an effect of the guidance of

[11] Joseph Cardinal Ratzinger, *Called to Communion: Understanding the Church Today* (San Francisco: Ignatius Press, 1996), 75-103.

the Holy Spirit in the Church. In the New Testament we see the beginning of Jesus Christ's provision of a universal pastor for His Church; thereafter, it took time to clarify that role, its fixed location, and its various responsibilities. The Anglican-Roman Catholic International Commission's *Final Report* of 1982 summed up the matter as follows:

> Though, it is possible to conceive a universal primacy located elsewhere than in the city of Rome, the original witness of Peter and Paul and the continuing exercise of a universal *episcope* by the See of Rome present a unique presumption in its favour. ... Therefore, while to locate a universal primacy in the See of Rome is an affirmation at a different level from the assertion of the necessity for a universal primacy, it cannot be dissociated from the providential action of the Holy Spirit.

The historical evidence that Peter journeyed to Rome, and eventually died there, is very strong. At the end of Peter's first epistle, for example, we read: "The Church, which is in Babylon ... salutes you: and my son Mark" (I Pt. 5:13). Babylon is a code word for pagan Rome. This much is clear from the Book of Revelation (where "Babylon" is used for pagan Rome six times), as well as from extra-Biblical works of the same era, such as the Syballine Oracles (5, 159 f.), the Apocalypse of Baruch (ii. 1), and 4 Esdras (3:1). According to the historian Eusebius, writing in about 303 A.D.: "it is said that Peter's first epistle, in which he makes mention of Mark, was composed at Rome itself; and that he himself indicates this, referring to the city figuratively as Babylon" (Hist. Eccles. 2, 15, 4.).

That Peter and Paul were the ones who founded and established the Church in Rome was well known to the early Christian writers. St. Irenaeus of Lyons, for example, bases his argument for Roman primacy on this undisputed fact (Against Heresies, 3, 1, 1, ca. 150 a.d.) Indeed, the early Christians also treated it as an undisputed fact that Peter was *martyred* in

Rome. The North African theologian Tertullian, for example, wrote: "How happy is that Church where Peter endured a passion like that of the Lord, where Paul was crowned in a death like John's" (De praesc. haer. 36, 1). Similarly, St. Peter of Alexandria, bishop of that patriarchal See, shortly before his death in 311, wrote the following words: "Peter, the first chosen of the apostles, having been apprehended often and thrown into prison and treated with ignominy, at last was crucified in Rome" (De paen; canon 9). Eusebius confirms the witness of Tertullian and Peter of Alexandria when he writes: "Nero is the first, in addition to all his other crimes, to make a persecution against the Christians, in which Peter and Paul died gloriously at Rome" (*Chronicles,* 68). Even as early as the end of the first century, St. Clement, the third Bishop of Rome, alluded to the "perseverance even to death" of the apostles Peter and Paul in his own city (I Clement 5:1-6). In addition to all of this evidence from Christian literary sources, we have a letter written at the end of the 3rd century by Macarius Magnes, an anti-Christian, pagan author, ridiculing the martyrdom of Peter and Paul of Rome, and we also have the modern archaeological excavations under St. Peter's Basilica in Rome, where evidence of Peter's ancient tomb has been uncovered.

All this is of some importance because if St. Peter died in Rome, it was most likely in that city that a succession to the Petrine leadership ministry and teaching tradition was passed down. Indeed, Pope St. Clement of Rome tells us that before they died, all the apostles appointed persons to continue their ministry — and St. Clement had been taught the Faith by the apostles themselves!

In addition, we have to consider all the practical difficulties involved if the Church had a mere "floating" primacy, which might have resided in Rome for a time, then have passed to Constantinople, and possibly to Moscow, and then elsewhere. When and where should this "floating" headship move? And who should decide? Could this not lead to endless, divisive disputes? How then could the universal pastorate be very effective in keeping the Church in a unity of truth and love? For example, the Orthodox theologian Afanassief argued that only the local church which "presides in love" should have "priority" over the other churches. Yet how are the local churches to know for sure which church is presiding in this way at any given time? Surely, this is just a recipe for ecclesiastical chaos! Of course, we always pray that the Vicar of Christ, the universal pastor, will preside in love. But Catholics argue that this pastorate belongs in the See of Rome by divine providence. If the successors of St. Peter are forced into exile, and dwell in exile even for many years, yet they retain the office of "Bishop of Rome," because it is in Rome that the succession to Peter's leadership ministry and teaching tradition was passed down, and because that succession was recognized, in various ways, by ancient ecumenical councils and many of the greatest Church Fathers. It is to the witness of those ancient Fathers and Councils that we must now turn our attention.

The Witness of St. Ireneus and St. Leo the Great

If the Petrine Ministry was given to us by our Lord Jesus Christ to serve and secure the Church's unity in truth and love, then we would expect to find, in the ancient and relatively undivided Church, under the guidance of the Holy Spirit, a nearly unanimous testimony to the existence of a universal pastorate centered in Rome, and an ever increasing clarity about its role and responsibilities.

By and large, Catholics argue, this is precisely what we do find.

One of the earliest witnesses to Roman pre-eminence was St. Ireneus. Born and raised in the East in the mid-second century, Ireneus learned the faith from St. Polycarp, who had known the apostle John personally. Ireneus later became bishop of Lyons in Gaul, thereby uniting East and West in his own person. As bishop, he argued vigorously against the Gnostic heretics that authentic Christian teaching would most likely be evident in those churches founded directly by the apostles, with a succession of bishops traceable back to that foundation. Among these churches, he held the Church of Rome to be pre-eminent, for it was founded by the two most glorious apostles; it was therefore the shining example and trustworthy standard of orthodoxy in the world (Against Heresies, 3,3,2):

> Since, however, it would be very tedious in such a volume as this, to reckon up the successions of all the churches, we do put to confusion all those [heretics]... by indicating that tradition derived from apostles, of the very great, the very ancient, and universally known church founded and organized at Rome by the two most glorious apostles, Peter and Paul ... For it is a matter of necessity that every church should agree with [or resort to] this church, on account of its pre-eminent authority, that is, the faithful [from] everywhere, inasmuch as the apostolic tradition has been preserved continuously by those [faithful persons] who exist everywhere.

This passage has been the focus of many scholarly disputes over the years. Perhaps the most effective challenge to Roman Catholic interpretations was given by the Anglican F. W. Puller in his work *Primitive Saints and the See of Rome* (1914). He sums up his own interpretation for us as follows:

> He [St. Ireneus] refers first to the various churches all over the world as manifesting the apostolic tradition. Then, to save time, he selects three of the apostolic churches as spec-

imens of the rest, and first of all he refers with special emphasis to the very great and very ancient Roman Church, and he says that to it, because of its more influential primacy, the faithful come flocking in from all quarters, and that the apostolic tradition is preserved in the Roman Church — by whom? By the infallible pope? No! By these Christians who have come to Rome from the other local churches.[12]

However, Puller's reading of this passage, still leaves us with the question: *why* do the faithful from all over the world so frequently come to Rome? Clearly, they do so on account of its "pre-eminent authority" ("propter potentiorem principalitatem," perhaps "pre-eminent firstness"). And why does the Roman Church have this pre-eminent place? If we follow St. Ireneus' line of argument, the answer can only be: because the public tradition of teaching in that See was founded by "the two most glorious apostles, Peter and Paul," and is therefore pre-eminently trustworthy. So the proper interpretation of this passage hinges upon why St. Ireneus might have regarded SS. Peter and Paul as "the two most glorious apostles." It cannot be that he held Rome to be unique in having two apostolic founders rather than one, because elsewhere in his book Ireneus mentions that Ephesus also had two apostolic founders: St. John and St. Paul. Moreover, there is no clear indication in the text that Ireneus held the teaching tradition of the Roman Church to be pre-eminent simply because the city was a centre of civil power or Christian pilgrimage. Such arguments appear nowhere else in St. Ireneus' writings, and in fact would intrude a new and (in the case of civil power, secular) line of reasoning into his overall argument for the doctrinal trustworthiness of the apostolic sees of Christendom. St. Ireneus holds that all the apostolic sees are trustworthy centres of orthodoxy because of their apostolic foundation and continuous teaching tradition, but above all

---

[12] F. W. Puller, *Primitive Saints and the See of Rome* (London: Longman's and Green, 1914).

the Roman See, because of its special and pre-eminent apostolic foundation. In this St. Ireneus agrees with his near contemporary Tertullian, who traces the pre-eminence of Rome not to civil power or devout pilgrimage, but to its special apostolic roots: "O Church, happy in its position... into which Apostles [Peter and Paul] poured out, together with their blood, their whole doctrine" (Praesc. haer. 36. 1).

In short, Rome is not said to be pre-eminently trustworthy by Ireneus because Christian pilgrims *bring* the true faith there; rather, faithful Christians resort to Rome because they know for sure that they will *find* the true, apostolic tradition preserved there, stemming from SS. Peter and Paul, the two most glorious apostles. Rome is thereby the principal reference point, the touchstone, of Christian orthodoxy.

Clearly, for St. Ireneus the Roman Church does not err in apostolic teaching. Moreover, for St. Ireneus, the bishops in each church are "those to whom [the apostles] committed the churches." Thus, he wrote at the end of his list of the early popes: "In this order and by this succession the ecclesiastical tradition from the Apostles and the truth has come down to us" (Adv. Haer. III, 3. 3). We may take it as implicit in St. Ireneus' thought, therefore, that the Bishop of Rome, as guardian of the trustworthy teaching tradition founded by Peter and Paul, is the trustworthy custodian of the apostolic truth passed down in that pre-eminent church.

Unfortunately for us, St. Ireneus did not speculate as to how this "pre-eminent authority" of Rome might operate in a real "crisis situation." Like St. Cyprian of Carthage a few generations later, he remained confident that disputes which arose in the universal Church could be settled charitably in the Holy Spirit, through the worldwide consensus of the fellowship of bishops (Adv. Haer. I. 10. 2). It seems he could not envision the possibility of the great sees of apostolic foundation "falling out" with one another on matters of faith — or at least not falling out for very long.

We shall return to St. Ireneus in this regard later.

Jumping ahead several centuries to the middle of the fifth century A.D., we find just such "crisis situations" emerging again and again, threatening to tear the Church apart. Even the great apostolic sees are now "at each others throats," so to speak, with the bishops failing to reach agreement among themselves, even in ecumenical council. In this situation, both East and West looked to the Roman See to help settle their disputes, and to preserve the universal Church in a unity of truth. For example, at the Council of Chalcedon (451 A.D.) it was the dramatic insistence of Pope St. Leo the Great that settled the controversy over the two natures of Christ, human and divine.

The Council's proceedings were opened by the papal legates who said that they were authorized by the Bishop of Rome, who is "head of all the churches," to demand that the heretical bishop Dioscorus should not attend, on the grounds that a few years earlier he had "presumed to hold a council without the authority of the Apostolic See, which had never been done nor was it lawful to do." However, the Council allowed Dioscorus a fair trial before deposing him on these, among other grounds. During the debate over the doctrine of Christ's two natures, Bishop Peter of Corinth crossed over from the side of Dioscorus and placed himself with the opposite party. These (mostly Eastern) bishops received him with the words "Peter thinks as does Peter; orthodox bishop welcome." The assembled bishops then accepted Pope Leo's view on the vital doctrinal issues in question with the common shout "Peter has spoken through Leo." Later, at the absolute insistence of Pope Leo, and under the threat of the withdrawal of papal support for the whole council, the Eastern bishops (i.e. all but four of the 600 bishops present), quite against their wishes, were compelled to compose a new definition of faith conforming to Leo's doctrine.

John Henry Newman argued that Pope Leo "forced" his views on this Council, "tyrannizing" over it, and trampling upon the most sacred traditions of Egypt. We should soften Newman's words, however, and admit that to some extent this "tyrannizing" was not fully allowed him (see, for example, the dispute over the final canons of the Council). To the extent it was allowed, it probably owed as much to the support of the Emperor's representatives at the Council as to any clear consensus at the time among Eastern bishops on the *precise* nature of papal primacy and its Petrine foundation: "Peter thinks as does Peter ... Peter has spoken through Leo." Nevertheless, after the termination of the Council, the Patriarchs of Antioch, Jerusalem, and Constantinople addressed a joint letter to the Pope, acknowledging him as "constituted interpreter of the voice of Blessed Peter," and as "the very one commissioned with the guardianship of the vineyard by the Saviour." "You indeed," they wrote, "as the head among the members, presided here in the person of your representatives."[13] In the Byzantine liturgy, therefore, on the feast of Pope St. Leo the Great, all the faithful sing: "As the successor of the divine Peter, enriched with his presidency and primacy, Leo published his divinely inspired definition."

---

[13] As quoted in Clement C. Englert, C.SS.R., *Catholics and Orthodox: can they unite?* (New York: Paulist Press, 1961), 99-100.

It is clear that in this critical instance of divisive contro-versy among bishops gathered in ecumenical council, the Roman See, in the name of its specifically Petrine teaching authority, prevailed against the inclinations of the vast major-ity of Eastern bishops and metropolitans. It did so to main-tain the Church in truth and unity. It did so even though the secular power of the city of Rome had long since declined; the barbarians had captured the city and the imperial capital had long since moved to the east. It is hardly fanciful to see here the hand of the Holy Spirit, guiding our Lord's Church to understand ever more clearly the role the Petrine Ministry might play in uniting in truth and love the fellowship of Christians throughout the world.

The Ancient Consensus

Thus far we have taken two examples, two snapshots, if you will, of the views of the early Christians regarding Roman Primacy. First, we looked at the view of St. Ireneus of Lyons, very much a mainstream and revered teacher of the 2nd century. Then we considered Pope St. Leo the Great and the Council of Chalcedon in 451 A.D. These two snapshots capture for us, at two early stages of the life of the Church, her developing mind regarding the proper role and authority of the continuing Petrine Ministry. Gradually, we see the Church, led by the Holy Spirit, unfolding and unpacking the meaning of the commission given to Peter, and what it implies for the life and mission of the Church to have a Christ-given rock and shepherd, a universal pastorate, in her midst. We see these implications unfolding in the face of various threats to the Church's unity and doctrinal integrity in the ancient world.

However, it is not my intention to outline for you a com-plete history of the early development of the papacy. Our aim in these chapters is more doctrinal than historical. We are laying foundations. To that end, the question that concerns us is to what extent there was any *consensus* among the ancient Christian saints, Fathers, and Councils regarding the Petrine Ministry. After all, the Eastern Orthodox tradition, (and to some extent the Anglican tradition too), has always been committed to the consensus witness of the ancient, relatively undivided Church as the best commentary on, and the best interpreter of, the original apostolic deposit of teaching and practice. Similarly, the Catholic Church does not allow her theologians to interpret scripture "contrary to the unanimous consent of the Fathers" (Vatican Council I). *Was there any unanimous (or nearly unanimous) consent among the ancient Fathers and Councils regarding Rome's Petrine Primacy?*

Many Catholic theologians have argued that there was such a consensus — and a highly significant one at that. Let me list for you three points on which there was nearly unanimous agreement among the ancient Fathers and Ecumenical Councils of the first eight centuries. These three points form the foundation of all subsequent developments of the papacy.

(1) The Roman Church under the pope was believed to be *the touchstone of orthodoxy*: the trustworthy guardian and repository of the apostolic faith because of its special Petrine foundation and ministry. *Rome has never erred in its official, definitive teaching of the Faith* — this was the common belief of most early Christians, at least until the late 5th century, and by almost all of the Church Fathers and saints until the 9th century.

(2) The Roman Church under the pope always manifested a *universal, pastoral concern* for the Church, sometimes writing to churches or bishops in far away places to approve or admonish them, and sending charitable aid to churches in distress.

(3) The Roman Church under the pope was seen as a *universal court of appeal* in matters of doctrine or discipline that seriously divided the churches, especially with regard to disputes in or over the other leading patriarchal sees, and disputes in the college of bishops, even in ecumenical council.

In the western Church, the papacy claimed, and was gradually able to exercise, even more authority. But at least on these three points, there was general acceptance by both East and West throughout the Patristic era.

The Consensus in The East

In the East, there had always been at least an implicit recognition of these three forms of Roman Primacy. St. Clement, for example, a first century Bishop of Rome, who had learned the faith at the feet of the apostles themselves, intervened in the internal struggles of the Corinthian Church in Greece in 96 A.D. He reprimanded them for deposing their clergy, and insisted, under penalty of sin, that they restore their clergy to their rightful posts. St. Clement wrote (I Epistle 5):

> Because of sudden and repeated calamities and misfortunes, we think our attention has been slow in turning to the things debated among you.

Later he adds (I Epistle 59):

> If some are disobedient to the things He [Jesus] has spoken through us, they should know that they are enmeshing themselves in sin, and no small danger.

Passages such as these prompted Catholic scholar, Fr. William Most to write:

> No ordinary person, without authority, would want or need to explain his slowness in taking up a case in a distant place, nor

would he claim Jesus had spoken through him, so it would be wrong not to comply. [14]

In fact, this letter from Rome was held by the Corinthians in such high esteem that it was still being read in that church a generation later. The ancient Church historian Eusebius even records a letter from Dionysius, Bishop of Corinth, to Pope Soter (ca. 166-174) praising the Roman tradition of pastoral care for churches even in the East:

> For from the beginning it has been your practice to do good to all the brethren in various ways and to send contributions to many churches in every city. Thus relieving the want of the needy, and making provision for the brethren in the mines by the gifts which you have sent from the beginning, you Romans keep up the hereditary customs of the Romans, which your blessed bishop Soter has not only maintained, but also added to, furnishing an abundance of supplies to the saints and encouraging the brethren from abroad with blessed words, as a loving father for his children.

Pope Clement's intervention in Corinth — and its positive reception — is all the more remarkable when one considers that the pope was judging the Corinthian situation from far away, even though the great church of Ephesus, founded by St. Paul and St. John, was near at hand. Yet in the East, the respect of the Corinthians for the universal pastorate was not unique. The great martyr-bishop St. Ignatius of Antioch, for example, a near contemporary of St. Clement, referred to the Roman Church as "the church that presides in love" (Epistle to the Romans, introduction). The Byzantine liturgy would celebrate the liturgical feast of St. Clement of Rome with the words: "Peter, the Prince of the Apostles, left thee as a worthy successor of himself; after him thou didst rule the Church most capably."

---

[14] Fr. William Most, *Catholic Apologetics Today* (Rockford: TAN Books, 1986), 91.

The ancient church historian Eusebius tells us that in the last decade of the second century, Pope Victor "endeavoured to cut off the churches of all Asia [Minor], together with the neighbouring churches, as heterodox, from the common unity," because they refused to conform to the widespread Roman custom of celebrating Easter on a Sunday (Eusebius, *Ecclesiastical History*, V. 24). Many bishops at the time sharply objected to Pope Victor's heavy-handed policy, including St. Ireneus, "who, in the name of those brethren in Gaul over whom he presided, maintains indeed that the mystery of the Lord's resurrection should be celebrated only on the Lord's day; but he also becomingly exhorts Victor not to cut off whole churches of God, which preserve the tradition of an ancient custom ... for the peace of the churches" (V. 24). St. Ireneus evidently succeeded in changing the Pope's mind, for a more tolerant policy was restored. But we cannot help noticing from this account how St. Ireneus argued his case: "for the peace of the churches." Evidently, he did not question the Pope's authority to excommunicate the churches of Asia Minor. He did not say "You have no authority to cut off whole churches from the common unity." Rather, St. Ireneus exhorted Pope Victor to be lenient for the sake of "the peace of the churches."

The early Ecumenical Councils of the Church also accorded primacy to the See of Rome. Canon 6 of the First Ecumenical Council of Nicea (325 A.D.) listed the leading sees of Christendom as: Rome, Alexandria, and Antioch. The version of this canon preserved in Rome actually mentioned the "primacy" of the Roman See. This version was read aloud by the papal legates at the Council of Chalcedon in 451 A.D. and although the Greek bishops had a different version of the Nicene canon, the imperial commissioners, in summing up the matter, declared that it was clear from all that had been discussed that Rome held the primacy. In any case, according to an even later Ecumenical Council (The Sixth, in 680 A.D.) that first Council of Nicea was summoned by both the Emperor Constantine and Pope Sylvester together, and it is arguable that Bishop Hosius of Cordova presided over the Council of Nicea both as imperial and papal legate. The ancient Byzantine liturgy, at least, interpreted Hosius' presidency at that first Ecumenical Council as the moral presence of the pope ("Father Sylvester... thou didst appear as a pillar of fire, snatching the faithful from the Egyptian error and continually leading them with unerring teaching to the divine light.") The East also recognized the presidency of Rome at the Third Ecumenical Council, in Ephesus in 430 A.D., when St. Cyril, patriarch of Alexandria, received express permission from Pope Celestine to preside over that Council with papal authority. St. Cyril had appealed to Rome in his controversy with the heretic Nestorius, Patriarch of Constantinople. Cyril was quite clear that to make such an appeal to Rome in a crisis situation was an ancient custom of the churches (Ep. 11.1 and 11.7) and called the Pope "the archbishop of the whole world." (PG 77, 1040). We have already seen the Petrine Primacy accorded to Pope St. Leo by the Eastern bishops, both during and after the Fourth Ecumenical Council. As late as the 8th century we find Eastern defenders of the use of holy images such as Stephen the Faster complaining to the assembled bishops at the heretical Synod of Hieria (PG 100, 1144):

> How can you call a council ecumenical when the bishop of Rome has not given his consent, and the canons forbid ecclesiastical affairs to be decided without the pope of Rome?

In all these ways we see the Roman Primacy manifested in the earliest centuries of Christendom. To recap: Rome intervened by letter in far-away Corinth, an eastern diocese. The Roman See was recognized as "presiding" over the whole Church by a saintly martyr-bishop of Antioch (St.

Ignatius), and was recognized as having "preeminent authority" by a saintly bishop of Lyons (St. Ireneus, who was educated in the East). A saintly Patriarch of Alexandria (St. Cyril) calls the pope "archbishop of the whole world." The popes were acknowledged as presiding over the First, Third and Fourth Ecumenical Councils, and at the Council of Chalcedon in particular, the pope was recognized by all as having the preeminent voice and ministry of Blessed Peter himself. Again, all this evidence stems primarily from the Christian East.

Disputes over the eastern patriarchal sees were frequently appealed to Rome. St. Basil of Caesarea, for example, had nothing but personal disdain for Pope Damasus, and later despaired of any effective intervention by that Pope in the disputes raging at the time in Antioch. Nevertheless, he entreated Pope Damasus to send persons to arbitrate between the churches of Asia Minor with the words: "We are in no case asking anything new, but what was customary with blessed and religious men in former times" (Letter 70). In 341-342 A.D., Pope St. Julius protested against the heretical Eusebian party for deposing, without papal consent, the Patriarch of Alexandria, St. Athanasius: "Not so have the constitutions of Paul, not so have the traditions of the Fathers directed; this is another form of procedure, a novel practice ... Are you ignorant that the custom has been for word to be written first to us, and then for a just sentence to be passed from this place?" (quoted by St. Athanasius, from his Apologia 35, 4). St. Athanasius and Pope St. Julius evidently believed it to be the ancient tradition that disputes over the great sees of apostolic foundation should be referred to Rome for judgment. Their view that the Roman Church is the highest court of appeal in the universal church was implicitly recognized by Eastern Church historians Socrates Scholasticus, and Sozomen at the time, and received endorsement by the Western Synod of Serdica (343-344 A.D.), a synod ratified in the 7th century by the eastern churches at a council in Trullo (692 A.D.).

The consensus of the Eastern Fathers held that in matters of doctrine, the public teaching tradition of the See of Rome does not err. St. Epiphanius of Cyprus, for example, regarded the Roman Church as having preserved the apostolic rule of faith uniquely intact (Haer. 27, 6). St. Ignatius of Antioch also seems to have recognized the supremacy of the Roman teaching tradition. He wrote to the Romans: "You have never envied anyone; you have taught others, but I wish that what you enjoin in your teaching may endure" (Letter to the Romans, 3). St. Ephraim the Syrian (ca. 306-373), the great biblical exegete, summed up his understanding of the Petrine Ministry as royal steward of the doctrinal "treasures" of the Church in poetic words which St. Ephraim placed in the mouth of the Savior Himself (Homilies 4, 1):

> Simon, my follower, I have made you the foundation of the holy Church. I betimes called you Peter [Kepha, or Rock, in the original text], because you will support all its buildings. You are the inspector of those who will build on earth what is false, you, the foundation, will condemn them. You are the head of the fountain from which My teaching flows, you are the chief of My disciples. Through you I will give drink to all peoples. Yours is that life-giving sweetness which I dispense. I have chosen you to be, as it were, the first-born in My institution, and so that, as the heir, you may be executor of my treasures. I have given you the keys of my kingdom. Behold, I have given you authority over all my treasures!

Similarly, for St. Macarius of Egypt (d. ca. 390), one of the greatest of the desert Fathers, the Petrine Ministry is the successor to the teaching Chair of Moses and to the throne of the High Priest of the Jewish Temple (Homily 26):

> For of old Moses and Aaron, when this priesthood was theirs, suffered much; and Caiaphas, when he had their chair, persecuted and condemned the Lord. ... Afterwards Moses was succeeded by Peter, who had committed to his hands the new Church of Christ, and the true priesthood.

Blessed Theodoret of Syria, in his appeal to Pope St. Leo against the heretical Monophysites in 449 A.D., wrote (Ep. 116, to Renatus):

> That all-holy See has the office of heading the whole world's churches for many reasons, and above all others, because it has remained free of the communion of heretical taint, and no one of heterodox sentiments hath sat in it, but it hath preserved the Apostolic grace unsullied.

At the same time, St. Flavian, Patriarch of Constantinople, appealed to Pope St. Leo to settle the Monophysite controversy in the East once and for all:

> The whole question needs only your single decision and all will be settled in peace and quietness. Your sacred letter will with God's help completely suppress the heresy which has arisen and the disturbance which it has caused; and so the convening of a council which is in any case difficult will be rendered superfluous.

It was two years later, after the Council of Chalcedon, that the patriarchs of Antioch, Jerusalem and Constantinople addressed Pope Leo as "constituted interpreter of the voice of Blessed Peter," and "the very one commissioned with the guardianship of the vineyard by the Saviour." In the sixth century, the Byzantine Emperor Justinian expressed a similar trust in Rome's teaching authority. He wrote to the Patriarch Epiphanius of Constantinople that the Roman See was "the supreme pontificate," and "head of all the churches," and again (Codex Justiniani 1. 1, 7):

> We have condemned Nestorius and Eutyches, prescribing
> that in everything the churches of God must keep unity with
> the most holy pope and patriarch of elder Rome ... for we
> cannot tolerate that anything concerning the ecclesiastical
> order be left out of relation to the holiness of that church,
> since it is head of all the most holy priests of God, and since,
> each time that heretics have arisen among us, it is by a sen-
> tence and right judgment of that venerable see that they have
> been condemned.

In 680 A.D. the Sixth Ecumenical Council wrote these
words to Pope Agatho:

> And so we leave to you, the Bishop of the first See of the
> whole Church, what is to be done, you who stand on the firm
> rock of faith, and we gladly acquiesce in your letters of true
> doctrine ... which we acknowledge as prescribed divinely
> from the supreme peak of the Apostles ... Peter spoke
> through Agatho.

Among the ancient and holy Fathers of the East, few are
as revered today as the 7th century saint Maximus the
Confessor. But what was St. Maximus' attitude toward the
teaching authority of Rome? St. Maximus appealed to Rome
in the midst of his great dispute with the heretical
Monothelite party. He wrote: "from the incarnate Word's
descent to us, all Christian churches everywhere have held
and hold the great Church that is here [at Rome] to be their
only basis and foundation since, according to the Saviour's
promise, the gates of hell have never prevailed against her"
(Opuscula theo: PG 91, 137-140). Thus, along with his great
contemporary St. Sophronius of Jerusalem (Mansi X, 896c.),
St. Maximus claims that the Roman Church rightly has "the
power to command all the holy churches of God in the entire
world." The pope, as supreme possessor of the power of the
keys, has authority to judge questions of orthodoxy, opening

the gates of the Church to believers, and closing them to heretics (PG 63, 460).

I give you this brief survey of the attitude of the ancient East to the Roman Primacy in order to dispel a widespread misconception. The misconception is that the ancient Councils, and the holy Fathers of the East, knew nothing of the Roman Primacy save for a "primacy of honor." The facts, however, speak of far more than an honorific primacy. Almost everywhere, Rome was regarded as inerrant in its Petrine teaching tradition, and as a universal court of appeal in serious controversies regarding doctrine and jurisdiction. Of course, some have dismissed the evidence for this on the grounds that the oriental custom of flattery should not be confused with actual doctrinal opinion. On this argument Maximus, Theodoret, Basil the Great, Cyril of Alexandria, Flavian, the Fourth and Sixth Councils — were merely flattering and "buttering up" the pope with grand titles, which they did not really believe, in order to obtain papal favour. Let us remember, however, that these so-called "flatterers" were not just any orientals, but, in several instances, great saints and doctors of the Church. Moreover, if we are to dismiss their words to the popes as insincere and duplicitous, what are we to make of their effusive praise of the Blessed Virgin Mary? Is this too to be dismissed as insincere, oriental flattery in order to curry favour with the court of heaven? Why do we dismiss the one and take seriously the other? Besides, we have listed also many instances of Eastern respect for the Roman Primacy which do not come from letters addressed to the pope; I refer, for example, to the words of St. Clement, St. Ireneus, St. Epiphanius, St. Ephraim, Bl. Theodoret, the Emperor Justinian, and Stephen the Faster, (cited above).

Even as late as the 9th century, there were still great Eastern Fathers who respected the pre-eminent teaching authority of Rome. St. Theodore the Studite, for example, appealed to Rome in the midst of the second great Iconoclasm controversy. Writing to the Emperor he said: "If there is anything in the patriarch's reply about which your Highness feels doubt or disbelief ... you may ask the Elder Rome for clarification, as has been the practice from the beginning, according to inherited tradition" (Letter 2, 86, PG 99, cd. 1332 A). For Theodore, the pope is "first in rank" in the Church (PG 99, 1153), "the pure and genuine source of orthodoxy ... the distinct calm harbour for the whole church from every heretical storm" (PG 99, 1159).

A most remarkable expression of 9th century Eastern deference to the primacy and teaching authority of Rome comes from the greatest of Eastern missionaries, St. Cyril and St. Methodius. Fr. J. Michael Miller summarizes this for us in his book *The Shepherd and the Rock*:

> The apostles to the Slavs, Sts. Cyril (†869) and Methodius (†885), were evangelizing while controversy raged between patriarch and pope. Belonging to the ecclesiastical tradition of the Christian East, the two brothers were subject to the patriarch of Constantinople under whose aegis they had begun their mission. Even so, they considered it their duty to give an account of their missionary labour to the pope, asking him to confirm their work! The two brothers submitted to the pope's judgment "in order to obtain his approval for the doctrine which they professed and taught, the liturgical books which they had written in the Slavonic language and the methods which they were using in evangelizing those peoples."[15]

Sometimes, the Eastern Fathers accepted an implicitly pro-papal interpretation of the New Testament "Petrine texts." Thus,

---

[15] J. Michael Miller, C.S.B., *The Shepherd and the Rock* (Huntington, IN: Our Sunday Visitor Press, 1995), 128.

St. Epiphanius, St. Gregory of Nyssa, St. Basil of Caesarea, St. Cyril of Alexandria, St. Maximus, and Blessed Theodoret all interpreted "the rock" on which the Church was founded in Matthew 16:18 as Peter himself, the chief apostle. Of course, many of these same fathers, along with many other ancient fathers both East and West, interpreted the Petrine texts in a variety of ways. Thus, Epiphanius, Gregory of Nyssa, Basil of Caesarea, Cyril and Maximus also see "the rock" in Matthew 16:18 as Peter's faith, or as Christ Himself, the object of Peter's faith. We find multiple interpretations of Matthew 16:18 in the West as well. St. Augustine was confused; at various times he expressed different interpretations, and finally, in his book of *Retractions*, stated that of these meanings "let the reader choose the most probable." The exegesis of St. Ambrose, St. Hilary of Poitiers, and St. Jerome seems to be similarly varied, and there remains much controversy among Patristic scholars regarding the viewpoints expressed in the works of St. Cyprian of Carthage (more on that later). Suffice it to say here that this *variety* of interpretations need not worry us as long as we do not interpret them as *contradictions*. It is not very likely that people as learned and saintly as Epiphanius, Gregory of Nyssa, Basil, Cyril, Maximus, Jerome, Hilary, and Ambrose would publicly, unwittingly and blatantly contradict themselves on such an important matter. It seems more likely that they found several layers of meaning in the Petrine texts, interpretations held as complementary rather than contradictory. Peter is indeed the Rock of the Church, insofar as his ministry is built on faith in Christ and on the promises of Christ, who is the ultimate sure foundation of the Church. As one of the greatest of the Eastern Fathers, St. Basil of Caesarea, once wrote (Hom. 29, De Paenit.):

> Peter is made the foundation, because he says: Thou art Christ, the Son of the Living God; and hears in reply that he is a rock. But although a rock, he is not such a rock as Christ;

for Christ is truly an immovable rock, but Peter only by
virtue of that rock. For Jesus bestows dignities on others; He
is a priest and He makes priests; a rock and He makes a rock;
what belongs to Himself, He bestows on His servants.

The Consensus in the West

The ancient Western Church, by and large, was clear and
solid in submission to the Roman Primacy. For example, we
have already seen the claims made by saintly popes themselves about the Petrine Primacy: in particular Clement,
Stephen, Julius, Damasus, and Leo the Great. Moreover, the
Western Fathers were usually clear and explicit in their belief
that the Roman See is the living embodiment of the ministry
of St. Peter. Thus, in 449 A.D. St. Peter Chrysologus of
Ravenna warned the heretic Eutyches in a letter that "blessed
Peter lives and presides in his own cathedra and gives the true
faith to all who seek for it." St. Ambrose of Milan (d. 397)
saw the Bishop of Rome as pastor of the Lord's flock, and as
the unswerving exponent of the Church's true creed (Ep.
42,5), and advised that matters touching on faith and order,
and the mutual relation of the churches should be referred to
the Roman See for settlement (Ep. 56,7). In his letters concerning disputes in Antioch, he insisted that unity in the
worldwide church is ensured by communion with the See of
Rome, which has succeeded to the Petrine Primacy, "for from
her flow all the rights of venerable communion" (Ep. 11).

A near contemporary of St. Ambrose, St. Hilary of
Poitiers (d. 368) wrote to Pope St. Julius and expressed his
approval of the Synod of Serdica, and the appellate jurisdiction of Rome endorsed by that Synod:

And you [Pope Julius], most dearly loved brother, thought
absent from us in body, were present in mind concordant,

and will ... for this will be seen to be best, and by far the most
befitting thing, if to the head, that is to the see of the Apostle
Peter, the priests of the Lord report [or refer] from every one
of the provinces.

The primacy of Rome also plays a role in the thought of
St. Augustine of Hippo. In 416 A.D., in three letters regarding
the Pelagian heresy sent by the African bishops to Pope
Innocent I, St. Augustine joined them in acknowledging that the
Roman See possessed a trustworthy authority grounded in
scripture and extending over the whole world. Pope Innocent
responded to these letters as follows: "[The Fathers] did not
regard anything as finished, even though it was the concern of
distant and remote provinces, until it had come to the notice of
this See [Rome], so that what was a just pronouncement might
be confirmed by the total authority of this See, and thence other
Churches." St. Augustine's comment upon this letter amounted
to a full endorsement of its contents: "[Pope Innocent] in reference to all things, wrote back to us in the same way in which it
is lawful and the duty of the Apostolic See to write" (Sermon
186). Like St. Ireneus, St. Augustine believed that to be in the
Catholic Church is to be in communion with the Roman
Church, "in which the primacy of the apostolic chair has always
been in force" (Ep. 43, 7), for Christ "appointed Peter the head
of all so that he might be the shepherd of the Lord's flock"
(*Quaest. Veteris et Novi Test.*, 75).

St. Optatus of Milevis in North Africa (ca. 367 A.D.)
presents a similar point of view. The "chair of Peter" in the
See of Rome is the center of unity for the whole Church (The
Schism of the Donatists 2, 2):

> You cannot deny that you are aware that in the city of
> Rome the Episcopal chair was given first to Peter; the chair
> in which Peter sat, the same who was head — that is why he

is also called Cephas — of all the Apostles; the one chair in which unity is maintained by all. Neither do other Apostles proceed individually on their own; and anyone who would set up another chair in opposition to that single chair would, by that very fact, be a schismatic and a sinner. It was Peter, then, who first occupied that chair, the foremost of his endowed gifts. He was succeeded by Linus, Linus was succeeded by Clement ... Damasus by Siricius, our present incumbent ...

Meanwhile, St. Jerome, educated both in the East and the West, was especially loyal to the Petrine See. In his younger days (ca. 374-379 A.D.) he expressed this in a letter to Pope Damasus (Letter 15):

I follow no one as supreme leader except Christ only; hence, I attach myself in communion with your Beatitude; that is, with the See of Peter. I know that the Church is built upon this rock. Whoever eats a [Passover] lamb outside this house is profane. Anyone who is not in Noah's ark will perish when the flood prevails.

In his later years, writing of the Origenist heretic Rufinus, St. Jerome equates the Catholic faith with the Roman faith, and implies that those who do not hold the Roman faith are, ipso facto, heretics (c. Ruf. I, iv).

Catholic theologians argue, therefore, that in the ancient Church, both East and West, there was a general consensus about the Roman Primacy. That the Petrine See of Rome has never erred, and does not err in its doctrinal tradition was a common belief among the ancient Fathers and Doctors. Moreover, Rome exercised a universal, pastoral concern for the care of the churches, frequently sending letters to admonish or teach the brethren, and sending charitable aid to churches in need. Finally, Rome was everywhere seen as a court of appeal in matters of doctrine and jurisdiction that seriously divided the churches, especially when the world-wide college of bishops was divided, or there was a dispute in or over one of the other great patriarchal sees. *Clearly, this is more than a "primacy of honor." It is a primacy of apostolic headship, a universal pastorate.* Catholic apologists, from an excess of zeal, have sometimes argued that it was even more than that. It certainly was not less.

The Rise of Constantinople

Sadly, the Church of Jesus Christ has never been able to carry on its life and mission apart from the political realities of the world. The political powers ever attempt to intrude into the life of the Church, to corrupt her doctrines, compromise her pastors and prey upon her sheep. The story of the development of the papacy is no exception. Even as the whole Church was beginning to clarify, and fully appreciate, the implications of the Petrine texts, along with the need for a universal pastorate, seeds of disunity and dissension in the Church were already being sown.

The imperial status of the city of Constantinople strengthened throughout the 4th century. As the new, imperial capital, this younger and politically influential See began to serve a vital function as a focus of unity and cohesion for the churches of the East. At the Second Ecumenical Council in 381 A.D., the Eastern bishops agreed that "the bishop of Constantinople shall have rank after the bishop of Rome, *because it is New Rome.*" A similar canon was passed at the Council of Chalcedon in 451 (by only one-third of all the bishops at that council — after the rest had gone home!). The papacy fought hard against such canons, and refused to ratify them. For by the unscrupulous, these canons could be taken to mean that the great sees of Christendom should be ranked according to the *political* standing of each city, rather than according to their apostolic, and Petrine foundation. This, of course, the See of St. Peter would never admit. Nor was Rome alone in this protest. Alexandria, the See of St. Mark, supported Rome in the dispute, and it is worth noting that because of Pope St. Leo the Great's protest, the disputed canon from Chalcedon remained officially unrecorded in the East until the sixth century. Pope St. Damasus summarized the Roman-Alexandrian view in his famous "Decree of Damasus" of 382 (a decree which no Father of the Church, East or West, disputed at the time):

> Although all the Catholic Churches spread abroad through the world comprise but one bridal chamber of Christ, nevertheless, the holy Roman Church has been placed at the forefront not by the conciliar decisions of other churches, but has received the primacy by the evangelic voice of our Lord and Savior, who says: "You are Peter [etc.] ..." The first see, therefore, is that of Peter the Apostle, that of the Roman Church, which has neither stain nor blemish nor anything like it. The second see, however, is that at Alexandria, consecrated in behalf of blessed Peter by Mark, his disciple and an evangelist, who was sent to Egypt by the Apostle Peter, where he preached the word of truth and finished his glorious martyrdom. The third honorable see, indeed, is that at Antioch, which belonged to the most blessed Apostle Peter, where first he dwelt before he came to Rome ... .

There is something faintly absurd in the claim by some scholars that the See of Rome itself attained ecclesiastical preeminence as a result of the political standing of the city. After all, there were few communities in the ancient world which cared *less* for worldly and secular honors than the early Christian Church. All too frequently, the earliest Christians were the object of secular scorn and persecution stemming from old Rome. The last books to be written in the

New Testament even refer to pagan Rome derisively as the harlot "Babylon" (2 Pt. 5:13, Rev. 17:5). Thus, when the Eastern bishops more and more tried to elevate the See of Constantinople because it was the new imperial capital, this was surely a falling away from the most ancient tradition. The earliest tradition was to rank the churches in a hierarchy according to their special apostolic — and Petrine — foundation and teaching tradition rather than according to political status. We have already seen this as early as the second century in the writings of St. Ireneus, reaffirmed (as we have seen) in the uncontested "Decree of Damasus" (382 A.D.).

Unfortunately, the more politically influential the See of Constantinople became, and the more worldly and corrupt the Church as a whole became in its marriage with the Empire, so much the more did the argument for a solely politically-based church leadership tend to assert itself. Such worldliness gradually sank so deep that between 484 and 514 A.D., most of the Eastern hierarchs were not particularly distressed to find themselves out-of-communion with the ancient See of St. Peter. The dispute began when the Byzantine Emperor Zeno attempted to settle a doctrinal controversy in the worldwide Church by imposing acceptance of his own theological treatise called the "Henotikon." Rome, of course, was not about to compromise with this attempt by the Emperor to usurp Petrine teaching authority; the pope excommunicated the collaborators with imperial policy immediately. In the end, the "Acacian Schism," as it was called, was settled on terms largely favourable to the papacy. In a document entitled the "Libellus Hormisdae" (519 A.D.), the Eastern Emperor, patriarchs, and bishops signed the following profession (PG 63, 460):

> We cannot pass over in silence the affirmations of our Lord
> Jesus Christ, 'You are Peter, and upon this Rock I will build

my Church'... These words are verified by the facts. In the Apostolic See the Catholic religion has always been kept undefiled and her holy doctrine proclaimed. Desiring, therefore, not to be in the least degree separated from the faith and doctrine of that See, we hope that we may deserve to be in the one communion with you ..., in which is the entire and true solidity of the Christian religion: promising also that the names of those who are cut off from the communion of the Catholic Church, that is, not consentient with the Apostolic See, shall not be recited during the sacred mysteries. This is my profession, I have subscribed with my own hand, and delivered to you Hormisdas, the holy and venerable pope of the city of Rome.

Here we find, reaffirmed by the East, a summary statement of much of the ancient consensus. According to this historic document, the Church was given an enduring Petrine Ministry by Jesus Christ; as a result, the Petrine See is the centre of stability and unity in the Church and that See has never erred and does not err in her definitive teaching of the Faith. To be in the communion of the Catholic Church is to be "consentient [of a common mind] with the Apostolic See." It follows, of course, that the Church has a universal pastorate in the See of St. Peter, and that this See ought to have sufficient authority of jurisdiction to match her universal responsibility of securing the unity in truth of Christ's Church. Sadly, the subsequent history of the Church reveals that many of the Eastern bishops did not entirely think through the full implications of what they were signing. East and West continued to drift apart, and the ancient consensus of the Fathers — with all its implications — was gradually forgotten.

III. The Universal Jurisdiction
of the Successors of St. Peter

In the last chapter, I tried to summarize for you the Christian consensus of the first eight centuries regarding the Petrine Ministry. I argued that the ancient Fathers and saints generally believed that (1) the Roman Church under the Pope, as in a special sense the Petrine See, is the touchstone of orthodoxy; it had never erred and does not err in its official, definitive teaching of the Faith; (2) Rome always manifested a special pastoral concern for the universal Church; and (3) Rome is a proper court of appeal in matters of doctrine or discipline that seriously divide the churches, especially with regard to disputes in or over the other leading patriarchal sees, and divisive disputes in the college of bishops. To be sure, some zealous Catholic apologists have claimed that the Petrine Primacy was even more elevated than this: that it operated as a kind of "absolute monarchy." The facts, however, certainly do not bear out such extravagant claims. On the other hand, the facts also do not bear out the claims of many Eastern Orthodox apologists that the East always regarded the Primacy of Rome as no more than a "primacy of honor." Rather, the Petrine Primacy was, we may say, a primacy of apostolic headship and leadership, a universal pastorate, including appellate jurisdiction and a unique Petrine teaching authority. Such, I would argue, was the ancient consensus, before that consensus fully unraveled in the 9th century.

All this seems to be manifested in the reign of the holy and humble Pope St. Gregory the Great in the 6th century. On the one hand, Gregory believed that the See of Rome was of unique, Petrine authority: "I would rather die than that the Church of Blessed Peter should degenerate in my days" (Epp. lib, IV. 47). Indeed, he saw the other leading patriarchates of Christendom as sharing in a derivative way in the Petrine authority of Rome: "For he [Peter] himself exalted the See in which he both dwelt and laid down his life [Rome]. He himself adorned the See to which he sent his disciple the Evangelist [Alexandria]. And he likewise established the See in which, though afterwards he left it, he sat for seven years" [Antioch; see Epp. lib. VII. 40]. Thus, Pope Gregory did not hesitate to assert his authority over the Patriarch of Constantinople, John the Faster. When two presbyters under the Patriarch's jurisdiction appealed to Rome in 593 A.D., complaining of their ill-treatment at a heresy trial, Pope Gregory took up their cause, and repeatedly insisted that they be given a re-trial. He wrote at the time, "I know not what bishop is not subject to the Apostolic See" (Epp. lib. IX. 59), and with regard to the See of Constantinople: "Who will doubt that it is subject to the Apostolic See?" (Epp. lib. IX. 12). The Patriarch of Constantinople finally submitted to Gregory's protest, and sent a statement of the case against the two presbyters to Rome. The two were tried before a Roman synod, and one of them (named John) was acquitted. Pope Gregory later referred to the case in a letter to the Bishop of Ravenna: "do not you yourself know that the suit of John the presbyter against John of Constantinople, our brother and fellow-bishop, came before the Apostolic See, and was settled by our sentence?" (Epp. lib. VI. 24).

On the other hand, it is fair to say that Gregory no more ruled the East as an absolute monarch than any of his predecessors had done. He unhesitatingly intervened in the East if anything was brought to his notice which seemed to call for it; but his interventions were rare and extraordinary. In the West, on the other hand, he governed and supervised on a regular basis. In the former case his action was exceptional and remedial; in the latter it was ordinary and executive. In the East he would intervene from without if things went wrong; in the West he liked everything to be done under his direct supervision, even when everything was going properly. Moreover, St. Gregory explicitly repudiated the title "Universal Bishop." From his letters, it is clear that he believed the title implied some kind of de-consecration of all other bishops, stripping them of their legitimate pastoral authority and "honor." He wrote: "if one be Universal Bishop, it follows that you are not truly bishops at all" (Epp. IX. 68). In short, what we see in St. Gregory's pontificate is an ultimately authoritative, yet as much as possible collegial expression of the universal, Petrine Primacy. Also, we see a difference between the type of jurisdiction the Pope regularly exercised over the Latin churches, and his rare and extraordinary interventions in the East.

There are some theologians who look back wistfully at St. Gregory's day, and wonder if East and West could not once again be reunited on such a basis. "If only the papacy today would be willing to return to that ancient consensus," they argue, "scale back its jurisdictional powers over the *whole* church, and limit them mostly to the Western patriarchate of Christendom ... ." Well, I shall comment more on these hopes later. Suffice it to say here that I do not share them. I believe the papacy attained its full jurisdiction, its full Petrine right of "apostolic intervention," as a proper development of what was *implicit* in the New Testament (the "keys"), from the beginning. The full Petrine ministry was therefore meant by Our Lord to extend over the *whole* Church, not just the western or Latin portion of it. The fact that by the Holy

Spirit the western part of the Church was first to fully appreciate the truth does not make this truth any less universal.

Before we proceed, however, we need to consider the writings of the one Church Father who most seriously challenged the universal jurisdiction of the See of St. Peter. I refer, of course, to St. Cyprian of Carthage.

The Challenge of St. Cyprian

Some scholars point to St. Cyprian as a decisive witness against the ancient claims of Rome. On the one hand, St. Cyprian vigorously resisted the baptismal policy of Pope St. Stephen. On the other hand, when St. Cyprian discovered that the Novationist heretics had established their own bishopric in the Eternal City, he wrote in a letter (Ep. 59 ad Cornelium, italics mine):

> Moreover, after all this, a pseudo-bishop having been set up for themselves by heretics, they dare to set sail, and to carry letters from some schismatics and profane persons, to the *Chair of Peter, and to the Principal Church, whence the unity of the priesthood took its rise*; nor do they consider that the Romans are those whose faith was praised in the preaching of the Apostle, and among whom it is not possible for perfidy to have entrance.

Again, in another letter Cyprian comments upon the selection of a new bishop of Rome (Ep. 53 ad Antonium, italics mine):

> Cornelius was made bishop of Rome by the judgment of God and His Christ, by the testimony of almost all the clergy, by the suffrage of all the people who were present at the time, when no one had been made bishop before him; *when the place of Peter and the Rank of the Apostolic Chair was vacant.*

For St. Cyprian, therefore, the "place of Peter" and the "Rank of the Apostolic Chair" was held by the bishop of Rome, and to that "Principal Church" due honour should be given. However, supported in his opposition to Pope St. Stephen's baptismal policy by his contemporary St. Firmilian (who, by the way, hailed from Asia Minor, center of resistance to Pope Victor's ruling on the date of Easter!), St. Cyprian evidently believed there was no need for a supreme *jurisdictional* authority to reside in any one see, since he held fast to the hope that all disputes could ultimately be settled by mutual charity and discourse in the worldwide college of bishops. Such optimism was still possible in the mid-3rd century! For Cyprian, therefore, the "place," "rank" and "principality" of the Petrine "chair" was a primacy of honor and influence rather than rule. In his treatise "The Unity of the Catholic Church," for example, he argued that as Peter was the first apostle to be given authority from the Lord, (Mt. 16:18), so Peter was the one from whom the unity of the episcopate took its rise, and in whom that unity was prefigured. For St. Cyprian, the honor and influence of Rome as the continuing presence of Peter in the Church — "The Chair of Peter and the Principal Church" — was therefore a living reality based on scripture. But with saintly optimism, Cyprian could not even consider the possibility that the principal sees of Christendom could one day fall out of communion with one another, or that many of them could be captured by heresy.

Both St. Cyprian and Pope St. Stephen were martyred before their bitter dispute over baptismal policy could be fully resolved. Implicit in St. Cyprian's writings, however, — albeit unconsciously implicit — was a full doctrine of the papacy. For the universal Church, ever threatened by divisions and disputes, *always* needs to have (in St. Cyprian's words) "the unity of its priesthood take its rise" from Peter. *And it can, and does continue to have that source of unity in Peter, down through the ages, because Peter's continuing presence and ministry in the Church ever lives in the See of Rome, in "the place of Peter and the Rank of the Apostolic Chair," as St. Cyprian wrote, in "the Chair of Peter and the Principal Church."*

The Scope of Universal Jurisdiction

Let us use the word "jurisdiction" to mean the authority necessary for the effective fulfillment of an office or ministry.

The question arises: given that Rome is the See of St. Peter, what form of jurisdiction should the Petrine Ministry possess if, with the help of the Holy Spirit, it is to be *effective* as the universal pastoral ministry, to strengthen and unify the Church in truth and love? In other words, if our Lord bestowed upon St. Peter the responsibility of feeding his sheep, the universal flock (Jn. 21:17), and unifying the Church as its "Rock" (Mt. 16:18), then what should be the nature and extent of the powers of this ministry, to enable the successors of St. Peter *effectively to fulfill these responsibilities?*

First of all, we need to remember from our study of the Gospel texts that Our Lord Jesus promised an unique ministerial commission to Peter in Matthew 16:17-19. He also summarized its essential nature for us. Peter was promised the power of the "keys," symbolic of the office of chief deputy of the king. His authoritative decisions to "bind" and "loose" — rabbinic terms for "forbid" and "permit" in the community of faith — were also to be ratified in heaven. *As these powers were given to Peter without any qualification, this surely implies that the fullness of supreme authority within the Church resides in the Petrine Ministry as chief deputy or chief "Vicar of Christ."* Moreover, this fullness of ministerial authority must extend over the whole, universal Church of Christ. Again, from our study of the scripture texts we saw that *the concept "shepherd" in Biblical times signified authority as well as tender care,* (2 Sam. 5:2; Is. 40:11; Ps. 77:20; 78:70-72; I Peter 5:2), *and Peter was called to be shepherd of the whole flock of Christ: "Feed my sheep"* (Jn. 21:17; Heb. 13:20). St. Bernard of Clairvaux (1090-1153 A.D.) summed up the implications of these Gospel texts in his *Five Books on Consideration*, addressed to Pope Eugene III:

> It is true that there are other doorkeepers of heaven and shepherds of flocks... (but) you have inherited a name more excellent than theirs. They have flocks assigned to them, one flock to each. To you all are assigned, a single flock to a single shepherd. Do you ask how I can prove this? From the word of the Lord. For to whom, and I include not only bishops but also Apostles, were all the sheep entrusted so absolutely and completely?

> If you love me, Peter, feed my sheep (Jn. 21:17). What sheep? The people of this or that city or region, or even of this or that kingdom? "My sheep," he said. To whom is it not clear that he did not exclude any? The Lord, entrusting all to one man, commended unity to all in one flock with one shepherd...

> Others are called to share part of the responsibility for souls; you are called to the fullness of power. The power of the others is bound by definite limits; yours extends even over those who have received power over others... Your privilege is affirmed, therefore, both in the keys given to you and the sheep entrusted to you.

Secondly, we need to bear in mind what I called in our first chapter a "remarkable scriptural fact." The fact is that *all* the authority that was promised to the apostles collectively *(Peter included), was initially and explicitly promised to Peter alone*. A few of the Church Fathers, such as St. Cyprian, interpreted this to mean that Our Lord used Peter merely to symbolize and prefigure the ministry to be given later to all the apostles. Yet there is really nothing we can point to in the New Testament that supports such a limited interpretation. It simply does not take into account all of the facts. For we see in Matthew 16 that Christ's commission to Peter is also highly *personal*, implying a unique ministry: only Simon Peter was given the "keys" to be the chief deputy of the king, and only he was named by Jesus "the Rock." From the wordplay used by our Lord, Peter himself, the Rock, is to be the rock on which the Church is built. As we have seen, this personal aspect of the text was also widely acknowledged by the Church Fathers. Moreover, only Peter was called to be the universal shepherd of the sheep in John 21.

For these reasons, the Catholic Church claims that we can only do full justice to *all* the ramifications of these Petrine texts if we interpret them as follows: *that Peter alone — as chief deputy of the king, rock of the church, and universal shepherd of the sheep — can sum up and exercise in his own ministry the ministry of all the apostles together (Peter included)*. This means that the continuing Petrine Ministry in the Church, living in the See of Rome, can exercise the same governing and teaching authority as the entire episcopate (with the pope) acting together. Thus, the successors of St. Peter can act in the name of the whole episcopate, and with the authority of the whole episcopate, but the episcopate cannot act to rule and teach authoritatively apart from the pope.

Third, the universal jurisdiction of the pope is a doctrine implicit in the consensus of the ancient Fathers and Doctors:

in their belief in the infallibility of the Petrine See in official matters of doctrine. If Rome is the very touchstone of Orthodoxy, as the ancient consensus held, then it naturally follows that the papacy should have full and immediate jurisdiction over every local church. In other words, *as the guardian and touchstone of orthodoxy, Rome must have the authority effectively to intervene wherever and whenever the fullness of revealed truth, or proper bonds of communion are perceived to be under threat.* For if the Bishop of Rome does not have the power to *secure* the Church in truth, then his charism of infallible proclamation of the truth is largely exercised in vain.

Finally, there is a clear and obvious practical need for a unifying, highest authority in the Church. Councils and synods certainly help with this; with the Petrine Ministry consenting and participating, they can be vital means to unify the Church in truth and love. Councils and synods, however, can be divided into factions (national, ethnic, economic, political or doctrinal); they can fall apart in disputes. A universal primate, on the other hand, *unites the Church under his indivisible person, as visible head of the Body, and solid Rock of all the Churches.* As Fr. Kenneth Baker wrote in *Fundamentals of Catholicism*:

> Peter is the Rock of stability on which Jesus built His Church. If there were doubt about the source of divine authority in the Church, it would soon splinter into many locally autonomous groups, with no central head. In fact, that is what happened to the Protestants once they separated themselves from the Chair of Peter.[16]

For reasons such as these, the First Vatican Council (1870) attributed to the Bishop of Rome "universal," "ordinary," and "immediate" jurisdiction over every Catholic

---

[16] Kenneth Baker, S.J., *Fundamentals of Catholicism,* vol. 3 (San Francisco: Ignatius Press, 1983), 114.

Christian, lay and ordained. As Vatican II put it (Dogmatic Constitution on the Church, "Lumen Gentium," no. 22):

> In virtue of his office, that is as Vicar of Christ and pastor of the whole Church, the Roman Pontiff has full, supreme, and universal power over the Church. And he can always exercise this power freely.

> The order of bishops is the successor to the college of the apostles in teaching authority and rule; or rather, in the episcopal order the apostolic body continues without a break. Together with its head, the Roman Pontiff, and never without its head, the episcopal order is the subject of supreme and full power over the universal Church. But this power can be exercised only with the consent of the Roman Pontiff. For our Lord made Simon Peter alone the rock and keybearer of the Church (cf. Mt. 16:18-19), and appointed him shepherd of the whole flock (cf. Jn. 21:15 ff).

To be sure, the fullness of the Petrine Ministry was first appreciated primarily in the West. It was in the West, by divine providence, that the full implications of the Petrine texts were first clearly seen, unfolded, and put into practice. The pontificates of St. Clement, St. Julius, St. Damasus, St. Leo the Great, and St. Gregory the Great manifest this quite clearly. Nevertheless, at times the Eastern Fathers were not far behind in their thinking. We have heard, for example, the words of St. Athanasius, St. Epiphanius, St. Basil the Great, St. Cyril of Alexandria, Bl. Theodoret, St. Flavian, St. Maximus the Confessor, and St. Theodore the Studite, the Council of Chalcedon, and the "Libellus Hormisdae." A full doctrine of the Petrine Primacy is actually implicit in this ancient consensus.

The development of appreciation for the full Petrine Ministry, however, was hindered in the East by political complications. These included the divisive claims of the younger See of Constantinople, and the religious pretensions of the Byzantine Emperors. As a result, most eastern Christians were unable to accord any more universal jurisdiction to the Bishop of Rome than his role as an extraordinary court of last resort: in other words, as a court of appeal in matters of doctrine or jurisdiction that seriously divided the churches, especially with regard to divisive disputes in the worldwide college of bishops, and disputes in or over the other leading patriarchates of Christendom. A Petrine right of *apostolic intervention*, whenever and wherever the fullness of faith or proper bonds of communion might be in jeopardy, however, was generally not accepted by the East. Sadly, if the East lagged behind the West in its appreciation of the fullness of the Petrine Ministry, *the popes themselves must share part of the blame.* For they sometimes pressed their claims so arrogantly, wielded their authority so heavy-handedly, or intervened in eastern affairs so ineptly that they obscured the truth by their own sins (one thinks, for example of Pope Victor's heavy-handedness over the Asian customs for Easter, and the inept intervention of Pope Damasus in the disputes over the See of Antioch). There were even popes who came very near to espousing heresy. More on that later.

Not An "Absolute Monarchy"

The Catholic Church does not consider the Petrine Ministry to be an "absolute monarchy"; there are appropriate limits on papal action. The See of St. Peter, the visible head of the Church, does not absorb all other ministries in the Body of Christ, nor does it claim to be the source of all other ministries. For example, the Catholic Church does not teach, and has never taught, that the universal primate is the source from which diocesan bishops derive their episcopal consecration, or their divine commission to teach, govern and sanctify. Christian ministry, both lay and ordained, springs directly from Jesus Christ Himself. The same Christ who preached directly to the crowds, also chose apostles to be, in a special way, stewards of the household of God (Mt. 10:40, 18:18, 28:18-20; Mk. 4:34, 6:6 ff; Lk. 10:16, 12:42 ff, 22:30; Jn. 13:20, 20:21). The Petrine Ministry too springs directly from a special commission from Jesus Christ, who intended it to serve, strengthen, and unify all other Christian ministries. The Vatican therefore teaches that the See of St. Peter must respect local ministries, customs, and traditions, *provided that these do not contradict the fullness of faith, nor disrupt communion.*

The Second Vatican Council in its "Dogmatic Constitution on the Church" (no. 23) viewed papal jurisdiction through the lens of the "koinonia" model of the Church (as discussed in our second chapter). Theologian Richard McBrien sums up this aspect of the Council's teaching as follows:

> Insofar as the Church is a communion of churches, the papal office serves the unity of the Church as "the perpetual and visible source of and foundation of the unity of the bishops and the multitude of the faithful." The pope's primacy is a primacy of service, in service of unity. Insofar as the Church is a communion of churches, the papal office must respect the legitimate diversity of those churches, a collegial mode of decision-making, and the time-honored Catholic social principle of subsidiarity, which holds that nothing is to be done by a higher group, agency, or level of authority that can be done better or as well by a lower group, agency, or level of authority.[17]

In the area of "collegial decision making" for example, one thinks of the formation of the universal synod of bishops, which now gathers periodically in Rome to aid the pope in

---

[17] Richard McBrien, *Catholicism* (San Francisco: Harper, 1994), 758.

shepherding the universal Church. On a more regular basis, much of the governance of the Catholic Church takes place through the various Roman "congregations," consisting mostly of cardinals from various parts of the world. In the early Church, Rome usually acknowledged and respected a large degree of "subsidiarity" in its dealings with the great eastern patriarchates. Today new developments in the area of "subsidiarity" include the formation of regional and national episcopal conferences — developments not really "brand new," but something of a shift in emphasis from the more centralized patterns of recent centuries. However, some observers express legitimate concern that such national and regional conferences tend to exaggerate their own teaching authority, confusing the faithful and creating unnecessary tensions with the supreme, universal teaching office (called by Catholics the "papal magisterium"). There is also a danger that a spirit of divisive nationalism might re-emerge in the episcopal college, as has happened all too often down through history, and continues to plague the life of the Orthodox communion to this very day. For reasons such as these, the Code of Canon Law (1983) states that any teaching by a national or regional episcopal conference which is intended to bind the faithful must receive the consent of the Petrine See. In short, "getting the balance right" between Petrine leadership and authority, episcopal collegiality, and local subsidiarity, is no easy task, but proper balance is essential to the healthy functioning of the bodily organism, and the Body of Christ is no exception.

Again, there is renewed emphasis today on the fact that each bishop in his diocese is a pastor and vicar of Christ in his own right, and not a mere local official or delegate of the pope. It is a common misconception that the First Vatican Council in 1870 relegated the bishops to the role of mere ambassadors of the papacy. The charge was first made by the

German Chancellor Bismark in 1872. The German hierarchy gave a vigorous response to Bismark in their Collective Declaration of 1875, which was later commended and approved by Pope Pius IX. The bishops wrote:

> It is in virtue of the same divine institution upon which the papacy rests that the episcopate also exists. It too has its rights and duties, because of the ordinance of God Himself, and the Pope has neither the right nor the power to change them. Thus, it is a complete misunderstanding of the Vatican decrees to believe that because of them "episcopal jurisdiction has been absorbed into the papal," that the Pope has "in principle taken the place of each individual bishop," and that the bishops are now "no more than tools of the Pope, his officials, without responsibility of their own." According to the constant teaching of the Catholic Church, expressly declared at the Vatican Council itself, the bishops are not mere tools of the Pope, nor papal officials without responsibility of their own, but "under appointment of the Holy Spirit, they succeeded in the place of the apostles and feed and rule individually, as true shepherds, the particular flock assigned to them."

While bishops are not mere delegates or ambassadors of the pope, it is also important to remember that each bishop must remain in communion with the See of St. Peter, for Christ instituted the apostles as a single college with a common mission, with Peter as their head. As the *Catechism of the Catholic Church* puts it (quoting Vatican II, "Lumen Gentium" nos. 19 and 22):

> When Christ instituted the Twelve, "He constituted (them) in the form of a college or permanent assembly, at the head of which he placed Peter, chosen from among them." Just as "by the Lord's institution, St. Peter and the rest of the apostles constitute a single apostolic college, so in like fashion the Roman Pontiff, Peter's successor, and the bishops, the successors of the apostles, are related to and united with one another."

Thus, the bishops must remain united to the Petrine Ministry, the head of the college, for apart from papal consent they have no proper area of jurisdiction or canonical mission (Lumen Gentium 21, 24), nor any authority to bind the faithful with definitive teaching of the Faith. Moreover, in a grave situation, wherever and whenever the fullness of the Faith or proper bonds of communion are being threatened, the See of St. Peter can always intervene directly, with full authority, and can always act unhindered. For the successors of St. Peter have full, supreme, and universal ministerial authority in the Body of Christ.

Just as the Petrine Ministry does not usurp the rights and duties of the diocesan bishops, so it does not usurp the rights and duties of the ancient, eastern patriarchs. On the contrary, as the history of the early church shows, occasionally the popes acted to *secure and protect* the proper rights of the other patriarchs (e.g. when Pope St. Julius stepped in to restore the patriarchate of Alexandria to St. Athanasius, who had been unlawfully and unjustly deposed from his See). To maintain and protect the proper role and ministry of the eastern patriarchates is actually one of the duties of the universal pastor. Pope John Paul II, in his Encyclical on Christian unity *Ut Unum Sint* (1995), has even expressed the willingness of the Vatican to find a way of exercising the Roman Primacy which, "while in no way renouncing what is essential to its mission, is nonetheless open to a new situation" — this "new situation" being the ardent desire of Christians in general for unity, and especially the ardent desire of Catholics for reunion with the East (for more on this subject, see the Postscript). In any case, the great Council of Florence in 1439 sought to guarantee historic, patriarchal rights when it proclaimed:

> We declare anew the order of the venerable patriarchates, as transmitted in the canons: the patriarch of Constantinople is second after the most holy Roman Pontiff; third is that of Alexandria, fourth that of Antioch, fifth that of Jerusalem; *all of whose privileges and rights evidently remain intact.*

Read in this context, we can still welcome the clear and uncompromising definition of the Petrine Primacy given to us by that same Council of Florence:

> We define that the holy apostolic See and the Roman Pontiff have the primacy over the whole world, and that the same Roman Pontiff is the successor of St. Peter, the prince of the apostles, and the true vicar of Christ, the head of the whole Church, the father and teacher of all Christians; and that to him, in the person of St. Peter, was given by Our Lord Jesus Christ the power of feeding, ruling, and governing the whole Church, as is also contained in the acts of the Ecumenical Councils, and in the sacred canons.

Misgivings of a Convert

Personally, I have to admit that, at first, all the arguments from Scripture, Tradition, and Reason for the Petrine Primacy were not completely convincing to me. Born and nurtured in a Protestant home, and then serving as an Anglican pastor for five years, it took more than rational argumentation to wean me away from my roots. What was it that held me back? In the end, I had few doubts about the scriptural and patristic basis of the papacy. What held me back was something else: fear.

One of my fears centered upon the bold, and seemingly outrageous claim, made by Pope Boniface VIII, in 1302, in his famous Bull "Unam Sanctam" ("One and Holy"). The Pope wrote: "We declare, state, define, and pronounce that it is altogether necessary to salvation for every human creature to be subject to the Roman Pontiff." So everyone who remains out of communion with the pope will end up in hell; is that what the Catholic Church really means by Petrine Primacy?

This fear was relieved when I actually read the *context* of that papal statement. It occurs at the end of the document which begins: "We are obliged by the faith and hold — and we do firmly believe and sincerely confess — that there is one Holy Catholic and Apostolic Church, and that outside this Church there is neither salvation nor remission of sins." In fact, most of the ancient church Fathers, both East and West, taught the same thing: "outside the Church there is no salvation." By that they usually did *not* mean that only "card-carrying" members of the Catholic Church had any chance of getting to heaven. For the Fathers also generally taught that the true Church existed in some sense *from the beginning of the human race*. All who follow the truth and commandments of God, as far as they are aware of them, are, in a sense, part of the one, true Church. Hence, St. Justin Martyr in the second century taught that some before Christ were really Christians because they followed the "logos," the Divine Word, in their hearts (Apology 1.46 cf. Jn 1:9). This was also the view of St. Irenaeus (Against Heresies, 4.28.2), and St. Augustine (Epistle 102, Retractions 1. 13. 3). The Catholic Church continues to teach much the same thing. In 1863, Pope Pius IX wrote on this subject in his encyclical "Quanto Conficiamur Moerore":

> We all know that those who suffer from invincible ignorance with regard to our holy religion, if they carefully keep the precepts of natural law which have been written by God in the hearts of all men, if they are prepared to obey God and if they lead a virtuous and dutiful life, *can by the power of divine*

light and grace, attain eternal life. For God, who knows completely the minds and souls, the thoughts and habits of all
men, will not permit, in accord with His infinite goodness
and mercy, anyone who is not guilty of a voluntary fault to
suffer eternal punishment.

Thus, the Catholic Church teaches that those who remain
outside of the visible fold of the Vicar of Christ through no real
fault of their own are not beyond the workings of divine grace.
They may live beyond the reach of Catholic missions; they may
have had the Catholic Faith poorly presented to them. They
may have received divine grace from the Catholic inheritance
of Protestant or Orthodox churches, churches which retained
elements of Catholicism when they broke away from Rome
(eg. the sacrament of Baptism, the Holy Scriptures). In that
sense, these Christian communities are not fully "outside of the
Church," and many of their adherents are simply following as
much light and grace as they have, as best they can. They are
close to the Holy Spirit, who is the "soul" of the Church Body;
they are "ordered to" the Church in a spiritual sense, and walk-
ing in the way of salvation (In fact, a few great saints, such as
St. Cyprian and St. Meletius, actually died out-of-communion
with the papacy because of squabbles with the Holy See — so,
one can not only be saved, but even, in very rare cases, attain
sainthood in such a state!). The Vatican reaffirmed this teaching in 1949 in response to the famous Leonard Feeney case. Fr.
Feeney had been preaching that only actual members of the
Catholic Church can escape hellfire. In a letter of that year
from the Holy Office to the Archbishop of Boston, the Vatican
made it clear that in order to be saved all must be in some way
close to the Church, but actual membership is not absolutely
required. Provided that one is related to the Church in desire or
longing, even implicitly, and this desire is informed by super-
natural faith and love, one can be saved. On the other hand,

those who remain outside the Petrine fold *are in a condition of considerable danger* because they necessarily lack many great gifts and helps from God, and the fullness of revealed truth, which they can find only in the Catholic Church.

The bold statement by Pope Boniface VIII about needing to be subject to the pope for salvation, therefore, needs to be read *in context*. For the first sentence of this document shows that this statement about the papacy is an elaboration of the general teaching "outside the Church there is no salvation" — and we have seen what that teaching really means, both to the ancient Church Fathers and to the Vatican. In fact, the statement by Pope Boniface about the papacy comes word for word from St. Thomas Aquinas (Contra errores Graecorum 36: 1125), and the context of St. Thomas's statement again makes it clear that it is just a statement of the traditional "no salvation outside the Church" doctrine.

The new Catechism of the Catholic Church, following the express teaching of the Second Vatican Council, continues this same interpretation of the "outside the Church, there is no salvation" doctrine (Catechism 847, Lumen Gentium 16):

> Those who, through no fault of their own, do not know the Gospel of Christ or his Church, but who nevertheless seek God with a sincere heart, and, moved by grace, try in their actions to do his will as they know it through the dictates of their conscience — those may achieve eternal salvation.

So much for my first fear. All my Protestant family, and my Anglican and Orthodox friends are *not* necessarily going to hell. Some of them are growing in grace. My job is to love and respect them, to pray for them, and to share with them the fullness of Catholic truth, as best I can.

A second fear, however, was just as strong in me as the first. The Catholic Church, it seemed to me, is a community governed too much by papal power, in direct contradiction of Christ's teaching; for did not Christ teach us that the apostles must not "lord it over" one another as the Gentiles do (Mk. 10:42-45)? But gradually, I began to see that this was an unfair accusation. After all, the First Vatican Council tells us that a universal pastor is necessary "in order that the episcopate also might be one and undivided, and that by means of a closely united priesthood the multitude of the faithful might be kept secure in the oneness of faith and communion" ("On the Church of Christ," introductory paragraph). So this was no "power-grab" by the papacy. The intention was not to "lord it over" anyone, but to secure the unity in truth and love of Christ's Body on earth, a unity for which our Savior had so earnestly prayed before His passion. The lack of that unity is a scandal to the world, as well as the chief obstacle to Christian evangelism. The universal pastorate was founded by Christ to be the servant of the Church's unity. Besides, the universal pastorate, if it is to manifest the shepherding of Christ, can no more be a pastorate devoid of the effective exercise of authority than was Christ's own ministry. Christ did not repudiate Messianic authority; He merely repudiated *wrong notions* of that power, for example, by rejecting the expectation of the Jews that their Messiah would be a violent, revolutionary leader. Christ Jesus *exercised divine power in loving service*. Hence, Our Saviour gave commands, issued rebukes, and drove out demons. Moreover, he left delegated authority (exousia) in the hands of His apostles (see Mt. 28:18-20).

My favorite portrayal of the unity in the Petrine Ministry of effective power and loving service comes from Karl Adam's classic work *The Spirit of Catholicism*:

Papacy and episcopacy are divine power, but power put to the service of love. Certainly the pope has sometimes to speak out in sharp and peremptory admonition. It is as when Paul cried: "shall I come to you with a rod?" (I Cor. 4: 21). And sometimes his anathema rings throughout the world "in the same tones and with the same language..." as St. Paul used when he excluded the incestuous Corinthian from the Christian community. Nevertheless, even this angry and corrective love remains love, love for the community of the brethren. The pope has in so far the primacy of love. Nor is there any hierarchy in the Church that may express itself otherwise than in ministering love. Woe to the pontiff who misuses his primacy of love for personal ends, to gratify his lust for power, his avarice or other passions! He sins against the Body of Christ, he offers violence to Jesus. He has to render an account beyond that required of any other members of the Body of Christ. How terribly at the judgment may the words stand in his ears, when the risen Lord shall ask him: "Peter, lovest thou me, lovest thou me more than these?" That is the great and sacred privilege of his office, to love Christ and His Body more than all other men, to realize that honourable title which Gregory the Great assumed: "Servant of the servants of God" (Servus Servorum Dei). Pope Pius IX, in his first Encyclical, laid it down that those who preside are nothing but "servants of the general weal, servants of the servants of God, especially of the weak and needy, after the pattern of our Lord." The pope's office is essentially service of the community, love and devotion. And when we prescind from the office, when we consider only the personality of the pope or bishop, then there is no distinction of rank in the Church, then the saying of Jesus is true: "Ye are all brethren" (Mt. 23:8). In the same Encyclical Pope Pius lays stress on the point that "only in this kingdom is there a true equality of right, wherein all are endowed with the same greatness and the same nobility, being ennobled by the same precious Blood of Christ." In the Kingdom of Christ there is only one kind of nobility, namely nobility of soul. The wearer of the tiara is the rock of the Church, and has the charisma of that office not for himself, but for his brethren. For himself he has no greater

Christian rights and no lesser Christian duties than the poorest beggar in the streets. Indeed, he is especially in need of the mercy of God and requires the intercessions of his brethren. And if his conscience be burdened with sin, then he also must kneel at the feet of his confessor, who may be the homeliest Capuchin friar.[18]

Upon hearing my arguments for the universal jurisdiction of the pope, a good friend once asked me — "But what do you Catholics do about a *bad* pope?" Well, thanks be to God we have not had a really bad pope for several centuries. The present one, John Paul II, may even be a saint. If we do get a really bad one, then we must pray for him, we must love and respect him, and we must obey him, as long as he does not ask us to break one of God's commandments. As St. Robert Bellarmine once wrote: "If the pope commanded what is manifestly vicious or prescribed what is manifestly vicious, one should say with Saint Peter (Acts 5:29): 'We must obey God rather than men'" (Recognitiones de Romano Pontifice IV, v).

"But what do you do if he corrupts the Gospel?" my friend asked. That will be the subject of the next chapter.

---

[18] Karl Adam, *The Spirit of Catholicism* (London: Sheed and Ward, 1938), 50-51.

IV. The Infallibility of the Successors of St. Peter

For Protestant Christians, the doctrine of papal infallibility has long been seen as the most grave obstacle to Christian unity. With characteristic frankness, the Reformed theologian Karl Barth once wrote:

> Now appears the great — and perhaps, after all, the sole — question we have to address to the Roman Church: to what extent is the pope's infallibility not competing with that of Jesus Christ? To what extent does the authority of the church not take place of that of Jesus Christ?

Perhaps we had best begin by defining what we mean by "infallibility," for misunderstanding of this word has caused more than a little strain in Protestant-Catholic relations down through the centuries. The doctrine of the infallibility of the papacy does *not* mean that each pope is flawless. It does not relate to his personal habits. It does not ensure that he is virtuous or prudent. It does not even mean that he will always speak up for the truth when he ought to. Finally, it does not mean that he is inspired as were the apostles; thus, the pope cannot write scripture, and cannot add any new revelation to the truth once and for all delivered to the saints (Jude 3). Rather, *the charism of infallibility is a negative gift, a negative protection*. In the words of Catholic apologist Karl Keating, papal infallibility means that

> Through the guardianship of the Holy Spirit, the Pope is guaranteed not to teach error regarding faith or morals (presuming, of course, he intends to make an *ex cathedra* statement and is not speaking as a private scholar). But he cannot

teach what is true unless he first knows what is true, and he learns that the same way we do.[19]

In other words, when the pope addresses the whole church, in an official, definitive teaching capacity as universal pastor and Vicar of Christ, Catholics believe that he is protected by the Holy Spirit from falling into error. Moreover, he is protected not by having a special "hot line" to the mind of God, but by the preventative, direct action of the Holy Spirit. The successors of St. Peter must *reach out for the truth* in the same way as any pastor or theologian, by prayer and study. But should they fail to fashion their mind or words properly, according to truth, then they are prevented by the Holy Spirit from definitively teaching or publishing error, and therefore stopped from leading the faithful astray.

The Scriptural Foundation

The basic principles behind the infallible teaching office of the Church as a whole stem from scripture itself. First of all, Christ Jesus promised the guidance of the Spirit of truth to His apostles (Jn. 16:13, 17:17). He authorized the apostles to teach with an authority similar to His own teaching authority (Lk. 10:16, Mk. 16:15), and His apostles believed that they had received that charism from His Spirit to help them guide and instruct the Christian community (Acts 15:28). St. Paul makes it clear that the charism of the Spirit of truth continues to abide in the Church when he writes of "*the church of the living God, the pillar and ground of the truth*" (I Tim. 3:15). Indeed, how could it be otherwise, since Christ Jesus Himself promised to be with us always, even to the end of time (Mt. 28:20), and since the Church is the very "Body" of the living Jesus Christ on earth (see I Cor. 12)? "You shall know the truth," Jesus promised, "and

---

[19] Keating, op. cit., 215.

the truth shall set you free" (Jn. 8:32). Scripture also teaches that the risen Lord is ever-present in the midst of His followers as the "Great Shepherd of the Sheep" (Mt. 18:20, Heb. 13: 20, I Pt. 2:25; 5:4). Although our Shepherd cannot always prevent us from falling into sin, His office as Chief Pastor surely implies that He does have the ability to prevent the consensus of His followers from corrupting the very apostolic gospel to which they were elected from all eternity to witness, and upon which they are to base their lives. Catholics would argue that if our Lord does not have the ability to do at least this much, then His Church certainly is not "the pillar and ground of the truth," and it ought not to be called the "Body" of the living Christ, and that Christ's office as "Great Shepherd of the sheep" is neither very effective nor very "great"! Despite His promise in Matthew 16:18, "the powers of death" would have prevailed against the Church and we would be wandering more or less in the dark.

It is for this reason that Catholics are deeply concerned by the teachings of some Protestant denominations. For even on their own reckoning, some of their distinctive doctrines were almost unknown in the Church from the time of St. Paul — or at the latest, St. Augustine — until the dawn of the Reformation over 1,000 years later. For example, where, in all that time, save for a few sects and individuals, do we find the belief that only "believer's baptism" is valid? Or belief in "double-predestination"? Or the belief that scripture is the sole rule of faith apart from the interpreting authority of consensus Tradition and the Magisterium of the visible Church? Christ promised that the "powers of death" would not prevail against the Church, but if these doctrines are true, then those powers did prevail, and the true Church was essentially dead for over a millennium!

Surely, this cannot be.

The Catholic Church therefore teaches that — at least as expressed in her official, definitive teaching voice — the Church of Jesus Christ has never and can never err in matters pertaining to faith and morals. The Church has no authority to *add* to the apostolic gospel, "the faith which was once for all delivered to the saints" (Jude 3), but the Church always *has* that apostolic gospel, and the Church also has the promise of the living presence of the Holy Spirit, the Spirit of truth, to enable her to interpret and define that gospel for the benefit of every generation.

Infallibility is therefore a charism which belongs, first of all, to the flock of Christ as a whole, both clergy and laity, the "sensus fidei" (sense of the faith), guided by the Great Shepherd of the sheep and His Holy Spirit in our midst. This charism enables the consensus of the Body of Christ truly to preserve and interpret the gospel. As Vatican II stated (Lumen Gentium 12):

> The body of the faithful as a whole, anointed as they are by the Holy One (cf. Jn. 2:20, 27), cannot err in matters of belief. Thanks to a supernatural sense of the faith which characterizes the People as a whole... in matters of faith and morals.

This infallible "sensus fidei" finds expression in an authoritative manner through the "moral unanimity," or consensus, of the definitive teachings of the Church's bishops around the world, in union with the pope (called the "infallible *ordinary* Magisterium"). On occasion, it is expressed through the definitive teachings of gatherings of bishops, in communion with the pope, in ecumenical council (Mt. 18:20; Acts 15:28). In addition, it can be expressed through official definitive pronouncements of the Petrine Ministry alone (these definitive papal and conciliar statements are called the "infallible *extraordinary* Magisterium"). In other words, this charism is expressed in a most trustworthy fashion through the hierarchical teaching ministry of the Church, although it is also true to say that whenever the Magisterium defines a matter of faith or morals infallibly, it does no more than give expression to the true understanding of the gospel, present implicitly or explicitly, in the mind of the faithful as a whole, clergy and laity together, down through the ages. For this reason, the First Vatican Council tells us that the infallible teaching authority of the See of St. Peter is an expression of that infallibility "with which the divine Redeemer willed *His Church* to be endowed." ("On the Church of Christ," chapter IV).

Eastern Orthodox Christians, along with some Anglicans, have often been willing to admit that the charism of "infallibility" is expressed through the authentic teachings of ecumenical councils. When the whole Church gathers together, in the persons of her bishops, to guard and define the Faith, then the Holy Spirit preserves the Church from grievous error. Some Eastern theologians also have been willing to admit that without the consent and ratification of the See of St. Peter, no council of bishops truly could claim the title "ecumenical." At any rate, as we saw in the second chapter, such was the general understanding of the ancient Church Fathers.

The Catholic Church, however, goes further. She teaches that the See of Rome, the See of St. Peter, is the very touchstone of orthodoxy: the trustworthy guardian and repository of the apostolic Faith, because of its special Petrine foundation and succession. In short, Rome has never erred in its official teaching of the Faith. Such is the claim of the Catholic Church; and as I argued in the last chapter, this, too, finds its echo in the witness of many of the ancient Fathers.

As we have seen, some of the ancient Fathers grounded this claim in the gospel Petrine texts. Fr. Kenneth Baker summed up the matter in his work *Fundamentals of Catholicism*:

> The New Testament does not say explicitly that Peter and his successors are infallible, but it most certainly implies it. Thus, Christ made Peter the rock-foundation of his Church, that is, the source of her unity and stability (Mt. 16: 18). *The unity (and stability) of the Church, however, is not possible without purity of faith, so Peter is the supreme and infallible teacher of the Faith.* Christ also gave Peter the power of binding and loosing, that is, the authority to declare and explain revelation.

In the chapter on scriptural foundations, we saw that the power to "bind" and "loose" meant the power to forbid and permit in the community of faith — *which included the ability to forbid and permit doctrinal teaching.* The exercise of these powers by Peter and his successors was also promised *heavenly ratification* by our Lord, *which surely implies infallibility* (Mt. 16:19). Baker continues:

> Jesus prayed that Peter should be strengthened in his faith and that he should *strengthen the brethren*: "I have prayed for you, Simon, that your faith may not fail, and once you have recovered, you in your turn must strengthen your brothers" (Lk. 22:32). Dangers to the Faith exist at all times, so *in order to fulfill this task properly, in matters of faith and morals the pope must be infallible.*

Furthermore, *Jesus chose Peter and his successors to "feed" his sheep* (Jn. 21:17), *to feed them with the gospel truth.* Now we know that it is possible for individuals, parishes, dioceses, even whole regions of the Church to fall away from the apostolic Faith. But if the Petrine Ministry could similarly fall away by teaching doctrinal error, it would mean not just the falling away of a single pastor, or a portion of the flock, but of the *universal* pastor. It would mean that the rock-foundation of the whole universal church could be "pulled out from under us," so to speak. Catholics do not accept that Christ Jesus would have built his Church on such a "shaky" foundation. Peter and his successors, as sinful men, are indeed sometimes as unsteady as the rest; but by the Holy Spirit, Christ preserves them from defining doctrinal error, making their ministry the rock of the Church, so that the multitudes of the faithful will not be led astray.

Finally, the New Testament tells us that Peter's commission was to focus and lead the authoritative teaching ministry given to all the apostles together. For example, Peter alone was given the ruling "keys," as chief deputy of the heavenly King, yet the apostles are said to share in powers of binding and loosing collectively, Peter included (see Mt. 18:18); Peter alone is called the "Rock" of the Church, yet the apostles and prophets together, Peter included, are called the foundation-stones (Eph. 2:10); Peter alone is given the charge to tend and feed the universal flock of Christ, yet all the church elders are seen as shepherds of the local flocks which they tend (I Pt. 5:2). In short, scripture shows that all the authority and ministry accorded to the apostles collectively, with Peter included, was initially and explicitly, and in a unique form, promised to Peter alone by Jesus Christ. As I argued in the last chapter, *the best interpretation of this scriptural fact is that Peter alone — as chief deputy of the King, rock of the Church, and universal shepherd of the sheep — can sum up and exercise in his own ministry the ministry of the whole apostolic band.* This means that the continuing Petrine Ministry in the Church, living in the See of Rome, can exercise the same governing and teaching authority as the entire episcopate acting together. Thus, the successors of St. Peter can act and teach, when the need arises, in the name of the whole episcopate, and with the authority of the whole episcopate, but the episcopate cannot act to rule and teach authoritatively apart from the consent of the Petrine Ministry, which is head of the apostolic band. It follows that if ecumenical councils of the episcopate teach and define the Faith infallibly, then so does the Petrine Ministry.

For these reasons, the Catholic Church teaches that the pope, as universal pastor and true Vicar of Christ, teaches infallibly whenever he speaks or writes with the intention of definitively binding the whole church on matters of faith and morals. His authority in such cases is equivalent to that of an ecumenical council, and entirely trustworthy. Indeed his ministry in this respect is an instrument and expression of the salvific ministry of the risen Lord Jesus Himself, the Great Shepherd of the sheep, preserving His flock from straying into grievous error, and feeding His flock with the truth of the gospel.

A Fanciful Spectre

The old spectre that haunts the imagination of Protestants, and many Eastern Orthodox, is that of an "absolutist" papacy: a central power that invents new dogmas of its own, claims divine inspiration for them, and imposes them upon the wider church. Yet, informed Catholics find this fear hard to comprehend. The infallible papal Magisterium does not claim to obtain doctrine by direct communication from God. Rather, it exists to serve the Church by unfolding, clarifying, and defining the apostolic deposit of Faith, thereby better expressing to the Church and to the world the historic Faith of the People of God. Moreover, the First Vatican Council specifically rejected the notion that the papacy has any authority to proclaim new doctrinal revelations (Dogmatic Constitution on the Church, Chapter four):

> For the Holy Spirit was not promised to the successors of Peter, that by His revelation they might make known new doctrine, but that by His assistance they might inviolably keep and faithfully expound the revelation or deposit of faith delivered through the Apostles.

According to Vatican I and its official expositors at the time, an *extraordinary,* definitive pronouncement of the Vicar of Christ can only be considered an expression of the infallible Magisterium of the Church when it manifests several characteristics:

> (1) it must directly concern a matter of faith or morals in such a way as to be related to the preservation, safeguarding, elaboration, or clarification of a truth of revelation; and

> (2) it must be expressly stated, or clearly implied, that the pronouncement is intended as "ex cathedra," in other words as a universal, permanently binding teaching.

Other principles of the Council were intended to guide the pope in the best way to form an infallible pronouncement. For example, the pope should first ascertain in some way the mind of the Church as a whole, especially her bishops and theologians, as well as the mind of the faithful everywhere. History shows that the popes did just that, in a most exhaustive manner, prior to their solemn decrees on the Immaculate Conception of Mary (1854) and the Assumption of Mary (1950). Moreover, any new definition must not contradict previous infallible teachings of the Church's Magisterium, such as previous definitive teachings of popes or ecumenical councils, or the clear testimony of Scripture. Indeed, any new definition must be rooted in Scripture, and in the witness of Christian antiquity, for these are the deep well-springs of faith, where the revealed truths of faith lie hidden, waiting to be drawn up into the clear light of day. The pope must therefore more clearly define, explain, or elaborate upon Scripture and the historic Tradition, drawing out its implications, but he cannot add new doctrines to the ancient deposit of the Faith.

Once an authoritative, infallible pronouncement has been made by the pope, it is important to bear in mind three things.

(1) The new definition does not require the formal consent of the bishops, or of the wider Church, in order to be free from error, because the definition already does and must express the consensus of the faithful down through the ages. This means that it will never be the imposition of something which the Catholic Church has not always generally, and at least implicitly believed. To the question "what if the pope formally taught heresy ex cathedra?," the Catholic answer is that the See of St. Peter has never done so, and would never freely do so, because the promises of Christ are true; His Holy Spirit always prevents the pope from definitively teaching error, keeping the Petrine Ministry as the "rock" of the faithful, and ratifying in heaven its acts of "binding and loosing." The hypothetical case of a pope defining heresy as truth, therefore, can never be more than hypothetical (more on this later).

(2) An infallible pronouncement of the pope is not preserved from error with regard to all the reasons, arguments and evidences given for the pronouncement, but only with regard to the central assertions of the decree itself. For example, Catholics may or may not be impressed with all the reasons given by Pope Pius XII for his solemn definition in 1950 of the Assumption of the Blessed Virgin Mary into heaven. Catholic theologians are free to debate these argu-

ments and evidences, and to try to improve upon them. But they must not cast doubt on the definition itself: that Mary really was assumed body and soul into heaven by our Lord.

(3) An infallible definition can be further elaborated or clarified by subsequent conciliar or papal teaching. Hence, "infallible" does not mean "completely clear," nor "complete in itself," and therefore an infallible definition need not be seen as "perfect" for every subsequent age. It may need to be drawn out, completed, or clarified in the future — without, of course, in any way contradicting it. The whole company ot the faithful has an important role to play here (again, more on that later).

It must not be supposed that the pope can teach authoritatively *only* on those rare occasions when he makes extraordinary, ex cathedra statements. Even in his ordinary encyclical letters, for the most part he reaffirms teachings already guaranteed by the infallible "ordinary Magisterium," or guaranteed by previous infallible definitions of popes and councils. Moreover, as Christ's own Vicar, and as supreme teacher and pastor of Christ's Church, even his technically "non-infallible" statements carry with them a strong presumption of truth. Often they can be shown to be expressions of the inerrant "sensus fidei" of the whole Church, down through the centuries, on matters of faith and morals, as found especially in the teachings of her greatest saints and doctors, to which the popes constantly refer.

In addition, it must not be supposed that a pope can only define a doctrine infallibly when he finds a near consensus present on the matter in the mind of the *contemporary* Church. For sometimes a pope may decide to act to *restore* an historic consensus on a matter of faith or morals which is being eroded. Pope Paul VI did this in his encyclical

"Humanae Vitae" on artificial contraception, and Pope John Paul II did so as well in his decree "Ordinatio Sacerdotalis" on the ordination of women. These documents reaffirmed historic Catholic teaching, and they irrevocably established that such teaching has been infallibly taught by the "ordinary Magisterium" of the Church down through the centuries.

Having clarified the teaching of the Catholic Church regarding the infallible teaching authority of the successors of St. Peter, let us move on to consider the principal challenges to this dogma, both from Catholic and non-Catholic sources. To a great extent, of course, I have already done this in our consideration of the scriptural and patristic basis of the Primacy of Peter, and the authority for ministry of the Petrine See. But now I need to respond to those challenges based not so much on Scripture or Tradition, but upon reason and logic.

The "Rationalist" and "Modernist" Challenge

I will call this the "Rationalist" and "Modernist" challenge because in essence it is a denial not just of the infallibility of the papacy, but a denial of any and every claim of "inerrancy" and "infallibility" in historic Christianity. This includes the inerrancy of the Bible (a belief which Catholics largely share with Evangelical Protestants) and the infallibility of the definitive teachings of authentic ecumenical councils (a belief which Catholics largely share with the Eastern Orthodox).

The Rationalist-Modernist attack was stated most succinctly by the American Anglican theologian Owen Thomas:

> The purpose of a claim of infallibility is apparently to offer *certainty of truth* in regard to the content of Christian faith. Thus, a statement by a putatively infallible spokesperson must

> be unmistakably clear, or else be infallibly interpreted by someone. Neither of these conditions is fulfilled in the case of papal infallibility. Moreover, the decision to accept the claim to infallibility is inevitably an act of individual judgment, which may be correct but cannot be known to be infallible.[20]

In the first place, as Cardinal Newman once pointed out, mental *certitude* should be distinguished from logical, mathematical *certainty*. The former is a matter of degree, a psychological exclusion of doubt, a subjective state produced by the convergence of many evidences and probabilities. In Catholic theology, this is sometimes called "moral certitude," just as in a courtroom we use the phrase "true beyond any reasonable doubt." For example, it was moral certitude, founded on overwhelming evidence, that enabled Peter to say to the crowds: "Let all the house of Israel therefore *know assuredly* that God has made him both Lord and Christ, this Jesus whom you crucified" (Acts 3:36). It is strong moral *certitude* — based on converging evidences from Scripture, Tradition and Reason — and not logical *certainty*, which any rational inquirer can attain with regard to the doctrine of papal infallibility. Moreover, as the doctrine of the Petrine Ministry is one of the truths of the Faith, no one can fully adhere to it on the basis of evidences alone; faith always comes by the special grace and action of the Holy Spirit (I Cor. 12:3, Eph. 2:8). This is called in Catholic theology "the certainty of faith."

Secondly, the decision whether or not to accept a particular doctrine as infallibly defined is not merely a matter of "individual judgment." As I shall argue in a moment, the pope, with the college of bishops, as successors to the full apostolic ministry, must ultimately be the ones to decide when the conditions for an infallible proclamation have been adequately fulfilled.

---

[20] Owen Thomas, *Introduction to Theology* (Harrisburg, PA: Morehouse, 1989).

Moreover, while some written papal or conciliar definitions may not be "unmistakably clear" in themselves, this does not mean they contain error. Catholic theologians insist that the whole company of the faithful has a role to play here. The Church as a whole must enter into the sense of an infallible definition to further clarify its language, draw out its meaning, pursue its implications, test the arguments which support it (without doubting the central assertion itself) and find the best way to integrate the definition into the whole body of Catholic doctrine. This is surely the way the Church grows into an ever deeper appreciation of the mysteries of Christ. This process goes on today with regard to the Marian dogmas (e.g., the contemporary debate about Mary's "coredemptive" role), and even with regard to the dogma of papal infallibility itself. Thus, while the label "infallible" enables us fully to trust the parameters and the wording of a particular papal or conciliar definition, it does not enshrine it as the "last word" on the subject, for the Church as a whole must use the definition to enter ever more deeply into the sacred mystery concerned, and this may one day give rise to an even clearer and more complete definition of the subject. For example, we can trace this process in the gradual apprehension and clarification of the doctrine of the person and natures of Christ in the ancient Church through the third, fourth, fifth, and sixth ecumenical councils.

Who decides whether or not a particular papal pronouncement is an expression of the Church's infallible Magisterium? Clearly, the papacy itself must make the claim to infallibility in each case. We must remember that Vatican I was careful to state that such papal teaching is infallible in itself, and not by consent of the bishops, or of the wider Church. The bishops cannot say, "we generally disagree with the wording or timing or content of this teaching, therefore it is not infallibly defined." What they might claim is that the conditions of infallibility were not adequately met in a particular case. Ultimately, the successor of St. Peter has the final say; he decides when the Church has made a solemn definition of faith or morals, and there is no need for further debate, for there is no higher court of appeal or judgment in the Church than the free, uncoerced judgment of the Petrine Ministry itself. If the pope rules that an infallible teaching has been made by the ordinary or extraordinary Magisterium, then the bishops and all the faithful must assent to the papal decree.

A similar question might be: who decides whether or not an episcopal council is truly "ecumenical" or not? First, of course, the council in some way would have to claim itself to be so. Second, the papacy would have to recognize and accept it as such, before any council of bishops could rightfully be accorded ecumenical teaching authority by the wider church, for the apostolic college cannot act authoritatively without the consent of Peter, the Bishop of Rome.

Those of a liberal-rationalist persuasion are usually fearful that acceptance of conciliar or papal "infallibility" leads the individual, and society as a whole, into a state of mental servitude: in our case, mental slavery to the pope. But this is far from the truth. The Catholic Church is a *voluntary* association; the Church has never definitively taught that people should be coerced into submitting to her hierarchy and her teachings. Over its 2,000 year history, there have been places where overzealous Catholics have assumed that coercion is a legitimate method for ensuring religious conformity (the Spanish Inquisition is the most notorious example), but such intolerance has been officially repudiated by

the Church on several occasions. The authentic Catholic attitude was enshrined in the famous Constitution of that most
Catholic of all nations, Poland, in 1791:

> The Holy Roman-Catholic Faith, with all its privileges and
> immunities, shall be deemed the dominant national religion
> ... but as the same holy religion commands us to love our
> neighbors, we therefore owe to all people of whatever per-
> suasion, peace in matters of faith, and the protection of gov-
> ernment; consequently we assure, to all persuasions and reli-
> gions, freedom and liberty. ...

It is nothing but a caricature of Catholicism to insinuate
that the papacy imposes upon the faithful a series of detailed
answers to all matters of faith and morals. Regarding most of
the mysteries of the Faith, while the Holy See sets firm
parameters, it also permits and encourages deeper explo-
ration of these mysteries, and recognizes differing schools of
Catholic thought concerning them (eg. the ongoing debate
between the Jesuits and the Dominicans regarding the mystery of predestination and election). If all this amounts to
mental "slavery" to the pope, it is a remarkably mild form of
intellectual servitude!

Universal Reception:
An Eastern and Anglican Challenge

The Eastern Orthodox tradition has generally held that
no doctrinal pronouncements by popes or councils can be
known to be infallible prior to their positive reception by the
wider Church. In short, the faithful as a whole, or at least the
episcopate as a whole, must give their consent, by recognizing such teaching as an authentic expression of the Faith that
they live and pray every day. Only then can we be sure that
the Church's pastors have defined the Faith infallibly, by the

Holy Spirit, the Spirit who fills the whole Body of Christ, not just the pope or the bishops in council.

In his book *Infallibility*, the American Roman Catholic Peter Chirico stated much the same thing. He argued that overt, manifest reception by the wider Church is required before any papal or conciliar teaching can be known to be infallible:

> The only way the Church can be sure that a pope or council has spoken infallibly is by finding the meaning proclaimed actually present in the consciousness of the faithful. Only when the vast numbers of the faithful discover that the meaning of a proclamation resonates with the meaning of the faith within them, and further, makes manifest this congruence of meaning explicit by word and implicitly by action — only then can the Church be assured that its authorities have spoken infallibly... only when infallible teaching has actually been received by the universal faithful can it be known to have been infallible.[21]

It is clear that the Anglicans of the Anglican-Roman Catholic International Commission (ARCIC) had something similar in mind. Summing up their deliberations on this point, ARCIC participants, E. J. Yarnold, S.J. and Henry Chadwick wrote:

> Anglicans it is true, would not take it for granted that a definition promulgated by the universal primate would be seen and held to be a matter of essential faith *before* the Church as a whole had entered into the sense of the definition, and perceived it to contain or to safeguard the truth of the Gospel (FR pp. 96-97). For Roman Catholics, on the other hand, once it is clear that the conditions [of infallibility] have been fulfilled, the definition is recognized as free from error.

All too often, the Catholic position has been caricatured by its opponents as somehow implying that the faithful as a

---

[21] Peter Chirico, *Infallibility* (Wilmington: Michael Glazier, 1983).

whole are to be mere *passive recipients* of papal and episcopal teaching. Yet I have already explained that such is not the case. Before exercising the infallible, extraordinary Magisterium, the pope (or council of bishops) is morally bound to listen to the mind of the wider Church, which always includes the Church of the *past* as well as the present, and certainly must not contradict any consensus of the whole Church, especially any consensus of the saints and Fathers. The wider Church also has a role to play afterwards in entering into the sense of an infallible definition, by further clarifying it and drawing out its implications. But Catholics argue that to make "universal reception" one of the criteria for discerning that the Magisterium has spoken infallibility is to *usurp part of the distinctive nature of the apostolic ministry of bishops.* The full apostolic ministry includes oversight in the Holy Spirit of the Church's teaching. As such, *the papacy and the episcopate must sometimes be able to teach something authoritatively which is not yet fully or explicitly appreciated by the wider, contemporary Church, even though it is already implicit in the Church's historic faith.* In such cases, the faithful have a Christian duty to assent to papal or conciliar teaching in the sense that they accept its parameters and wording as undoubtedly trustworthy and free from error, as far as it goes, and will faithfully use such teaching to enter more deeply into the sacred mysteries concerned.

As a matter of fact, this is precisely what happened at the first apostolic council, related in Acts 15. The apostles and elders in council debated, and then decided upon the question of the admission of uncircumcised Gentiles to the Christian community. Their final decision on this matter was explained in the letter that they sent to the Christians in Antioch, a letter that makes it clear that they were not waiting for their decision to be welcomed and "received" by the whole body of the faithful in order to know for sure that their decision was in accord with the Spirit of Truth. On the contrary, the council assumed that their decision already carried the authority of the Holy Spirit, and ought to be obeyed by the churches (15:28): "for it has seemed good to the Holy Spirit and to us to lay upon you no greater burden than these necessary things... ."

If the pope and the bishops do not have the authority in the Holy Spirit to call for such assent, then in what sense can they speak with decisive authority at all? Their teaching role would be reduced merely to "suggesting" or "proposing" doctrinal definitions to be held by the wider Church. They could not lead the way. They could not finally settle disputes. They would not be authoritative leaders or teachers in the Holy Spirit.

A serious practical objection to the Chirico-Anglican-Eastern position on "universal reception" also springs to mind. Simply put: in practice, it would be impossible to know when this condition actually had been fulfilled. For example, what proportion of the faithful would have to give assent to a solemn doctrinal definition before anyone could know it had been "received." Two-thirds? Three-quarters? And for how long? Fifty years? Three hundred years? A thousand years? And can the faithful withdraw their reception after a hundred years or so, if they change their minds? And how is reception to be measured? By opinion poll? By universal plebiscite? In practice, heretical propagandists could always claim that a magisterial definition with which they disagreed had not yet been fully "received" by the wider Church, and so lacked authority, or they could claim that the faithful were in the process of gradually withdrawing their assent. In short, *the teaching office of the Church could not effectively settle disputes, and unite the church in truth, if the criteria of "universal reception" were to be added to the teaching of Vatican I.*

It follows that the Chirico-Anglican-Eastern position cannot actually fulfill the theological understanding of the Church's teaching authority which was agreed by ARCIC. First of all, the Commission agreed that the Holy Spirit can be trusted to keep the Church faithful to the fundamental truths of the Gospel. They also agreed that it is the task of those who exercise authority in the church "to help produce this common mind," and that "for the Church to be preserved in truth in this way, there must be moments when it can be known to be preserved from error in defining essential doctrine." Yet as we have seen, the practical difficulties and unanswerable questions surrounding the doctrine of "universal reception" would make it virtually impossible for the believer to know if the Church had been preserved from error in its official, doctrinal definitions.

Some Orthodox theologians have limited the need for "reception" solely to reception by the universal episcopate; others limit the necessity of reception to the "pentarchy" the five ancient patriarchal sees (Rome, Constantinople, Alexandria, Antioch and Jerusalem). But it is not clear from history that the entire episcopate or pentarchy "received" some of the greatest ecumenical councils. The Council of Ephesus was certainly opposed by the Patriarch of Constantinople, Nestorius, who was deposed as a result; most of Syria and Egypt rejected the Council of Chalcedon. Therefore, how can universal episcopal or pentarchical "reception" be necessary before a conciliar or papal teaching can be known to be infallible?

It is only fair to point out that even in the Eastern Churches, some doubts have been expressed about "universal reception." Bishop Kallistos Ware drew attention to this in his popular book *The Orthodox Church*:

> To the question, how one can know whether a council is ecumenical, Khomiakov and his school gave an answer which at first sight appears clear and straightforward: a council cannot be considered ecumenical unless its decrees are accepted by the whole Church. Florence, Hieria, and the rest, while ecumenical in outward appearance, are not truly so, precisely because they failed to secure this acceptance by the Church at large. (One might object: what about Chalcedon? It was rejected by Syria and Egypt — can we say, then, that it was "accepted by the Church at large"?). The bishops, so Khomiakov argued, because they are the teachers of the faith, define and proclaim the truth in council; but these definitions must then be acclaimed by the whole people of God, including the laity, because it is the whole people of God that constitutes the guardian of tradition. This emphasis on the need for councils to be received by the Church at large has been viewed with suspicion by some Orthodox theologians, both Greek and Russian, who fear that Khomiakov and his followers have endangered the prerogatives of the episcopate and "democratized" the idea of the Church. But in a qualified and carefully guarded form, Khomiakov's view is now fairly widely accepted in contemporary Orthodox thought.[22]

Of course, the Catholic Church does not deny that those determined to remain in communion and concord with the successors of St. Peter will in fact "receive" papal and conciliar definitions as true (see Lumen Gentium no. 25). Moreover, as we have seen, the Catholic Church would not deny that the whole body of the faithful have a role to play, both in the formation of the Church's doctrine, and ultimately in the penetration and clarification of defined doctrine. What the Catholic Church has never taught is that "universal

[22] Ware, op. cit., 256-257.

reception" is needed for the *ratification* of the teachings of the Magisterium before they can be known to be infallible, for this would indeed usurp the apostolic authority of the Church's bishops. Moreover, as we have seen, this view is laden with severe logical and practical problems — problems so severe, in fact, that they completely undermine the ability of the Church hierarchy to teach with unifying and trustworthy authority.

Finally, we need to consider challenges to the doctrine of papal infallibility stemming from within the Roman Church itself.

Papal Infallibility: Infallibly Defined?

The Roman Catholic theologian Harry J. McSorley raised this question in the light of the famous statement by the Second Vatican Council that the Church of Jesus Christ subsists in, but is not co-extensive with, the Roman Catholic Church. As McSorley put it:

> If a dogma can only be considered infallible when it "embodies the Church's unanimity," to use Tavard's phrase, then it is possible, in the light of what Vatican II considers the *whole* Church to be that these dogmas are not infallible.[23]

Another way to express this would be to say that since the papacy is not infallible in its exercise of the power of excommunication, then it is possible that it has at times wrongly excommunicated branches of the Catholic body. In particular, one could argue that, in the eleventh century, the Eastern Churches were de facto excommunicated, but for insufficient reasons. As a result, this significant portion of the Church was not properly consulted with regard to the formation of the Vatican I decree on papal infallibility, nor

---

[23] Gregory Baum, et al, *The Infallibility Debate* (New York: Paulist Press, 1971).

properly represented at that Council, and so at least one of the criteria of infallibility was never met. And if Vatican I did not teach infallibly, then the dogmas which depend upon it are not yet infallibly defined either.

Perhaps the best way to answer such arguments is to consider the nature of the charism of infallibility itself. The guidance of the infallible Spirit of Truth is surely an abiding and essential mark of the Church. In other words, if the Church could fall into error concerning the fundamental saving truths of the Gospel it must live and preach, then this implies that it could one day lose the Spirit of Truth and, temporarily at least, cease to be the Church. Yet this can never happen, for Christ Jesus promised the everlasting guidance of the Spirit of Truth to His Church (Jn. 14:15-17, 16:13), promised to be with His Church *always* (Mt. 28:20), and promised that the powers of death would not overcome it (Mt. 16:18). It follows that the charism of infallibility, the Spirit of Truth, safely resides in the Church (I Tim. 3:15). If so, then the Church must never be able to lose such unity that it would no longer be able to exercise that charism.

One could then argue that even if the universal pastor wrongfully excommunicated sections of the Catholic Church, we can trust that under the guidance of the Spirit, the Petrine Ministry — the ministry established by Jesus Christ to serve the Church's unity — would never unjustly excommunicate such a portion of the Church that those left in communion with the See of Peter could no longer exercise the charism of infallibility. The division between East and West was a tragic wound to the Body of Christ, but it did not strip the Catholic Church of one of her essential marks: the apostolic truth, and the guidance of the Holy Spirit to preserve and interpret that truth aright for the sake of every generation. We need to remember that the charism of infallibility is a promise made to *the whole visible Church in its fullness*: that means to all those who remain in communion with the Petrine Ministry, the Church's rock of unity and stability, and in concord with the official, doctrinal "binding and loosing" authority of the Petrine See (Mt. 16:17-19; 18:18). Those lacking either in such communion, or such doctrinal concord, can still be termed "Christians," and can still receive many of the gifts and graces of the Spirit. But the gift of the *fullness* of revealed truth safely resides only in the fullness of the Church with the fullness of the means of grace: the Catholic Church united to Peter.

Within the Catholic fold, doubts about papal infallibility linger not so much for the clever, theological reasons of intellectuals. The real problem is that some Catholics see the doctrine as somehow "pre-Vatican II," a throwback to "the bad old days," or at any rate as somehow not in the "spirit of Vatican II," nor in the spirit of "renewal." Personally, I do not share the view that the period before Vatican II was a time of darkness — nor does the Magisterium! I doubt that many of today's so-called "liberal Catholics" have even read the documents of Vatican II regarding papal infallibility, for the fact is that Vatican II reaffirmed the teachings of Vatican I *in toto* — "rounding it out," so to speak, with further teaching on the role the college of bishops and the laity, without in any way contradicting what Vatican I had stated about the papacy. The relevant passage from the Vatican II documents is found in "Lumen Gentium" no. 25, and reads as follows:

> The infallibility with which the divine Redeemer willed His Church to be endowed in defining a doctrine of faith and morals extends as far as the deposit of divine revelation, which must be religiously guarded and faithfully expounded. This is the infallibility which the Roman Pontiff, the head of

the college of bishops, enjoys in virtue of his office, when, as the supreme shepherd and teacher of all the faithful, who confirms his brethren in their faith (cf. Lk. 22:32), he proclaims by a definitive act some doctrine of faith or morals. Therefore his definitions, of themselves, and not from the consent of the Church, are justly styled irreformable, for they are pronounced with the assistance of the Holy Spirit, an assistance promised to him in blessed Peter. Therefore, they need no approval of others, nor do they allow an appeal to any other judgment. For then the Roman Pontiff is not pronouncing a judgment as a private person. Rather, as the supreme teacher of the universal Church, as one in whom the charism of the infallibility of the Church herself is individually present, he is expounding or defending a doctrine of Catholic faith.

More recently, in the ecumenical encyclical "Ut Unum Sint," Pope John Paul II reaffirmed the teaching authority of the Bishop of Rome, and set it in the context of what is essential to the Petrine Ministry as a whole (no. 94):

The mission of the Bishop of Rome within the College of all the Pastors consists precisely in "keeping watch" (episkopein), like a sentinel, so that, through the efforts of the Pastors, the true voice of Christ the Shepherd may be heard in all the particular Churches. In this way, in each of the particular Churches entrusted to those Pastors, the *una, sancta, catholica, et apostolica Ecclesia* is made present. All the Churches are in full and visible communion, because all the Pastors are in communion with Peter and therefore united in Christ.

With the power and authority without which such an office would be illusory, the Bishop of Rome must ensure the communion of all the Churches. For this reason, he is the first servant of unity. This primacy is exercised on various levels, including vigilance over the handing down of the Word, the celebration of the Liturgy and the Sacraments, the Church's mission, discipline and the Christian life. It is the responsibility of the Successor of Peter to recall the requirements of the common good of the Church, should anyone be tempted to overlook it in the pursuit of personal interests. He has the duty to admonish, to caution, and to declare at times that this or that opinion being circulated is irreconcilable with the unity of faith. When circumstances require it, he speaks in the name of all the Pastors in communion with him. He can also — under very specific conditions clearly laid down by the First Vatican Council — declare *ex cathedra* that a certain doctrine belongs to the deposit of faith. By thus bearing witness to the truth, he serves unity.

The charism of infallibility, therefore, insofar as it resides in the office of the Vicar of Christ, is a gift of love bestowed by the risen Lord Jesus upon His Church for the sake of the unity, in truth and love, of His whole mystical Body. Through this gift of the Holy Spirit, the risen Lord Himself sanctifies His Body in truth, so that His followers may know the truth, the truth that sets them free (Jn. 8:32). The First Vatican Council expressed this beautifully in its decree "Pastor Aeternus":

> The charism of truth and of indefectible faith was divinely conferred on Peter, and on his successors in this chair, in order that they might fulfill their very exalted charge for the salvation of all men; in order that through them the whole flock of Christ might be kept away from the poisonous allure of error, and be fed with heavenly doctrine; finally, in order that, all occasion of schism having thus been suppressed, the whole church should be conserved in unity and, firmly resting on its foundation, should strongly resist the powers of Hell.

V. THE PETRINE MINISTRY:
YESTERDAY, TODAY AND TOMORROW

I have done my best in the preceding chapters to present the reasons why Catholics believe in the universal jurisdiction and infallible teaching authority of the Petrine Ministry. Even if I have not convinced you of the solid scriptural and patristic basis for these beliefs, I hope at least that I have cleared up any misunderstandings you might have had. Ecumenical dialogue, after all, begins with mutual understanding. Also, I hope I have demonstrated that Catholic theologians are not deaf to the challenges to their beliefs presented by Protestants, Anglicans and Orthodox, as well as by Liberals, Rationalists, and Modernists — and even so-called "liberal Catholics." I have tried to respond to these challenges along the way.

However, there is one group of challengers that I have more or less "left till last." These are the Church historians. I wrote a little about the early history of the papacy in the chapter on the Patristic era. However, there are some Church historians who have claimed they can *disprove* papal infallibility by pointing to the facts of history. To this latter challenge, therefore, we will now direct our attention.

Yesterday: A Fallible Papacy?
It used to be that anti-Catholic writers would point to changes in the Magisterium's teaching about usury as the best example of an error in official teaching. It was said that

up until the modern era, the papal Magisterium forbade all usury, whereas now it permits the lending of money with interest.

One needs to bear in mind, however, that the Latin word "usura" was a word of broad meaning, a word which could refer to charging interest in general, or to excessive interest, especially the lending of money at excessive interest to the poor. It is not clear that the Catholic Church ever meant to condemn all usury, in every circumstance. Fr. William Most explains:

> Looking at general moral principles, it is obvious that how much interest can be justified will vary with the type of economy. In some economies, money is virtually sterile; in others it is highly productive. Further, if there is a risk in a loan, more interest is justified.

> The Church has always understood this. Even back in the period envisioned by the objection, we find this distinction. Thus, the Fifth Lateran Council in 1515 taught: "This is the proper interpretation of usury [namely] when gain and increase is sought from the use of a thing that is non-productive, and with no labour, no expense, and no risk."[24]

More often than not, however, the historian's case against papal infallibility rests on the alleged, heretical teachings of individual popes. Three instances from the early church are usually brought forward. We shall look at each of them in turn.

(1) *Pope Liberius.* It is claimed that Pope Liberius compromised the orthodox Christian Faith in the Incarnation by signing an heretical statement of faith in 357 or 358 A.D. However, there were several mitigating factors in the event. For one thing, it is fairly clear that Pope Liberius was not act-

---

[24] Most, op. cit., 171-172.

ing as a free agent when he signed. He was at the time a pope-in-exile, deposed from his See for refusing to support the heretical Arian views of the Emperor. He was also a prisoner of the Emperor, and under threat of death from heretics and their supporters. For this reason St. Athanasius, the great champion of orthodoxy at the time, excused Pope Liberius with the words:

> But Liberius, having been banished, after a period of two years, succumbed, and, frightened by threats of being put to death, subscribed.
>
> Yet even this only shows their violent conduct, and the hatred of Liberius against the heresy, and his support of Athanasius, so long as he was suffered to exercise a free choice.

No contract signed under duress is binding, so whatever the Pope was forced to sign in such a situation is of no account. In addition there is also some doubt that the statement Liberius signed was unequivocally heretical. The document no longer exists, but, those who pressed upon Liberius to sign were mostly so-called "semi-Arians" who held to the vague formula that the Son is of "like substance" with the Father, which could be interpreted in both an heretical or an orthodox sense. Although some scholars argue that the document may have condemned the use of the Nicene word "homoousion" — "one substance" — with the Father, the document may have condemned it only in the way the word was used in the condemnation of heretics at the Council of Antioch in 268 A.D. Thus, it is not clear that Pope Liberius explicitly condemned an orthodox use and definition of the word.

Several years later, Pope Liberius refused to assent to an explicitly heretical Arian statement of faith adopted by the western council at Arminium, even though almost all of the other bishops of the West had bowed to imperial pressure to sign.

Doubtless, Pope Liberius was not as strong and courageous for the Faith as he should have been. But we can hardly charge him with freely and unequivocally rejecting the Catholic Faith in the Incarnation, much less with doing so with any intention to bind the faithful of the world to heretical teaching. Hence, *the case of Pope Liberius, in exile and under threat of death, pressured into signing a vague doctrinal formula, is no real argument against the Catholic belief that the successors of St. Peter, with the help of the Holy Spirit, are preserved from error when they freely and explicitly define the Faith for the whole Church.*

(2) *Pope Vigilius.* The case of Pope Vigilius is much more complex, but really has nothing to do with the infallible teaching authority of the Roman Pontiff. The whole matter has been adequately dealt with by many Catholic apologists and so I will do no more than repeat their words for you here.

First, Catholic author Karl Keating describes the situation for us:

> Emperor Justinian published a decree condemning the writings of three men long dead (Theodore of Mopsuestia, Theodoret of Cyrus, and Ibas). Their writings were known as the Three Chapters, and the heresy to which they subscribed was Nestorianism, which held that in Christ there are two persons joined together, God the Son and the man Jesus. (The orthodox doctrine is that there is only one Person in Christ, the divine, but two natures). Justinian's decree was designed to please the Monophysites. Monophysitism was a heresy that arose in reaction to Nestorianism; it held that in Christ there was only one nature, the divine. The decree was

signed by the Western patriarchs, but other bishops objected, saying the decree undermined the orthodox position by seeming to favor Monophysitism by default. At first [Pope] Vigilius refused to condemn the Three Chapters.[25]

Unfortunately, the Pope thereby incurred the wrath of the Byzantine Emperor. We will let Fr. William Most tell the rest of the story:

The Pope was arrested in 545 and taken to Constantinople. There he did agree to condemn The Three Chapters in 548. But then the Pope retracted the condemnation and refused to sign an edict by Justinian in 551 which condemned The Three Chapters. The Pope had to flee. Justinian proposed a Council, which was not to be truly universal but attended by only a few bishops from the East. The Pope did condemn the errors of Theodore of Mopsuestia and Theodoret of Cyrus, but let Ibas alone. Justinian was not content, so the Council condemned Vigilius until such time as he should repent. Of course, a Council acting without a pope has no validity at all. Yet, Vigilius broke under pressure, and did condemn The Three Chapters.[26]

It is important to note at this point that at *no time did Pope Vigilius ever teach or defend any of the heretical statements made by these three authors.* Karl Keating admirably sums up this whole incident:

The controversy concerned the expediency of condemning certain writings and of judging three men who had long since been judged by God. Vigilius intended to condemn only what was condemnable in the Three Chapters, not what was orthodox. The drawn out incident is certainly confusing, but it gives no support to the anti-infallibility position, since Vigilius never asserted that a heretical belief was to be believed as true[27]

---

[25] Keating, op. cit., 228.
[26] Most, op. cit., 213.
[27] Keating, op. cit., 228.

(3) *Pope Honorius*. This is sometimes held to be the strongest card in the anti-Catholic deck. Pope Honorius, it is said, not only taught heresy, but was condemned as a heretic by an ecumenical council of the Church. Yet once again, on closer inspection, the case against the papacy is extremely weak. Honorius is alleged to have expressed heretical opinions in letters written to the Patriarch of Constantinople in 634 A.D. — *but no one has ever claimed that the pope is infallible in his personal or private letters to another patriarch!* The Catholic belief is that the successors of St. Peter are necessarily preserved from error when they teach and define the faith with the intention of binding the universal Church for all time on a matter of faith or morals. Theological speculations or opinions — even strongly held beliefs — expressed to another patriarch by private letter are not "ex cathedra" statements of the See of St. Peter, that is, not unless it can be shown that the Pope intended such letters to be widely published, and accepted by all the faithful.

Moreover, the fact that the Third Council of Constantinople (680 A.D.) presumed to condemn Pope Honorius for heresy on the basis of these letters 42 years after his death is of little consequence. It is possible, of course, that a pope could hold and even express heretical opinions, and in that sense, truly be called a "heretic." He could do so, for example, in speaking to a limited audience, or in his private correspondence, or over the breakfast table. In any case, *no council of bishops has authority except insofar as its decisions are confirmed by the Petrine Ministry, and the successors of Pope Honorius certainly did not ratify his condemnation by the Council.* They rejected the claim that Honorius was a heretic, and with good reason, as we shall see. The most that Rome would admit was that

Honorius had neglected his duty by failing to recognize heresy clearly, and to denounce it when it rose up before him. Once again, this is no argument against papal infallibility, because *no one has ever claimed that the pope is infallible when he chooses **not** to define or condemn a doctrine.*

Did Pope Honorius express heretical opinions in his letters? I seriously doubt it. In a brilliant article in *This Rock* magazine (September, 1994), Catholic apologist Robert Spencer shared the fruits of his research on this matter, from which I shall now quote at length. Spencer writes:

> Sergius was another one of those stalwart patriarchs of Constantinople, anathematized for originating the Monothelite heresy. Monothelitism was one of a series of attempts to reconcile the Monophysites who, at that time were a huge portion of the Christian world, with the Catholic Church they had torn by schism more than two hundred years previously.
>
> The Monophysites maintained that our Lord's human nature had been absorbed into his divine nature. They could not accept the decree of the Council of Chalcedon (451) that "the only-begotten Son of God must be confessed in two natures, unconfusedly, immutably, indivisibly, inseparably united... without the distinction of natures being taken away by such union."
>
> Sergius, the first Monothelite, tried to effect a compromise by teaching that our Lord had only one will, a divine will. Like many compromises, this one ultimately pleased no one. To the orthodox it was anathema, for it denied the fullness of Christ's human nature. To Monophysites it was no more welcome, for this will-less but otherwise intact human nature which Monothelitism attached to Christ seemed to them to deny his unity.
>
> None of this was clear in the palmy days of 634. Monothelitism had encountered some criticism from the prescient Patriarch of Jerusalem, Sophronius, but elsewhere it

was more politely received. The Pope had not yet heard of it. With evident high hopes in his own inventiveness and craftiness, Sergius wrote to Honorius about his thoughts.

In his two letters, Sergius warned that teaching two wills in Christ would lead to the idea that the human will of the Son of God was opposed to that of his Father. He advised the Pope that it was better to speak of only one will in our Lord. Sergius was trying a little sleight of hand: He was attempting to deny the existence of Christ's human will by pointing out that our Lord never opposed the Father. Yet if two persons agree, they may be spoken of as being of "one will"; this doesn't mean, of course, that one of them has no will at all.

The Pope, with no idea of Sergius' *between-the-lines message* answered the Patriarch on the unthinkable subject of Christ's "opposition" to the Father. "We confess one will of our Lord Jesus Christ, since our (human) nature was plainly assumed by the Godhead, and this *being faultless, as it was before the Fall.*" Since Christ's human will is "faultless," there can be no talk of opposing wills. (Christ hardly would have been faultless if he opposed his Father's will.)

Monothelites, as they grew in numbers and influence over the ensuing years, seized upon Honorius' confession of "one will of our Lord Jesus Christ" as confirmation that the Pope believed with them that Christ had no human will. Newman and other commentators have noted that Honorius' letters to Sergius are not doctrinal definitions ex cathedra; thus they are outside the scope of infallibility defined by the First Vatican Council.

That is true, but, even more to the point, a look at Honorius' exact words shows that while he did use a formula — "one will" — that was later declared heretical, he used it in a sense that implied the orthodox belief.

This was picked up as early as 640 by Pope John IV, Honorius' successor, who pointed out that Sergius had asked only about the presence of two *opposing* wills. Honorius had answered accordingly, speaking, says Pope John, "only of the human and not also of the divine nature." Pope John was right. Honorius assumed the existence of a human will in Christ by saying that his nature is like humanity's before the Fall. No one would claim that before the Fall Adam had no will. Thus Honorius's speaking of Christ's assumption of a "faultless" human nature shows that he really did believe in the orthodox formula of two wills in Christ: one divine, one human, in perfect agreement.

The Third Council of Constantinople was thus in error when it condemned Honorius for heresy. But a Council, of course, has no authority except insofar as its decrees are confirmed by the pope. The reigning Pontiff, Leo II, did not agree to the condemnation of his predecessor for heresy; he said Honorius should be condemned because "he permitted the immaculate faith to be subverted."

This is a crucial distinction. Honorius probably should have known the implications of using the "one will" formula; he could have found out by writing a letter to Sophronius of Jerusalem. But he was no heretic.

The anti-papists got the wrong guy. It seems incredible that so many readers of Honorius's letters, from Patriarch Sergius to Hans Küng, *see only what they want to see* in Honorius's "one will" formula. We should thank God that *this poor old pope saw fit to explain himself.* Rarely outside of the homoousios/homoiousios controversy at the First Council of Nicaea has so much hinged on so few words.

Since this case seemed to be the best one the anti-infallibilists could turn to, I became an infallibilist, a Catholic with faith in the pope as the Vicar of Christ and successor of St. Peter. The Church will live beyond the trials of these days as it did those of Honorius's day. That bare fact may seem abstract and impenetrable in the convulsions of our age, yet it is our unshakable guarantee.[28]

---

[28] Printed with permission from Catholic Answers.

Today and Tomorrow

Some years ago, I had a friend with whom I would "talk theology" over coffee at a local café. He had the rather unnerving habit of interrupting me, in the midst of my long elocutions on ecumenism, with the melancholy words: *"For God's sake, let's talk straight; we're dying men you know."* Over the years, I have come to appreciate the wisdom of those words more and more. In ecumenism in particular, there is often a need to cut through all the rhetoric with some "straight talk." On the one hand, we tend to whitewash over our real differences with an overly vague use of words and concepts, only to congratulate ourselves at the end of the day with being "one in the Spirit" (as if the Spirit were not really the "Spirit of *Truth*" — as if our Lord had never said "You shall know the *truth*, and the truth shall set you free"!). On the other hand, and at the other extreme, there are those of us whose sole contribution to the quest for reunion is to spray all the rest of us with ignorant cultural or ethnic pride. As I began this book with some honest, straight-forward talk, therefore, I want to finish it the same way. After all, I am a dying man, talking to dying men and women, and at the end of the day we have an account to give.

First of all, if you are a theologian, or a theology student, I want to ask you if you opened this book with an honest, inquiring heart. We theologians, you know, have some characteristic sins which we do not often like to face. One of our most grievous sins is that after years of deep, professional, theological study we tend to tie things up in a neat package and stick a label on it entitled "my theology" — with special thanks to Barth, or Rahner, or Moltmann, or whomever. As a result, though St. Paul pleaded with us to be all of one heart and one mind, the community of theologians today, I'm sorry to say, is a veritable cacophony of private theologies, each one jealously guarding his own fragments of truth, his own "package," and each one's perspective distorted by his own characteristic sins and cultural biases. Therefore, I am asking you, at this point, if you read the words in this book with a truly honest and inquiring heart, or were you tied up inside your "package" the whole time? Of course, one should have an honest and inquiring heart before reading *any* set of sincere Christian reflections — but I'm making a special plea for you to examine your conscience this time. It is not only because I believe these chapters cover a most important topic for ecumenism. The papacy, after all, is either the great center for Christian unity, or its greatest stumbling block. But it is not only the *importance* of the topic that leads me to exhort you in this way; it is also the *danger* of this topic. What I mean is, if the Catholic teaching about the Petrine Ministry is true, then *all our little "packages" ultimately have to go*. We should no longer have "your theology" and "my theology," and endless, gentlemanly debates between us. Rather, we must freely surrender to the *Church's* theology: to the mind of the Church in the Holy Spirit, as expressed by the Catholic Magisterium, a clear and consistent light for nearly two millennia. Our little personal "packages," then, must be freely let go, and we must allow the light from our limited, personal perspectives to be completed and corrected by the common light of the "consensus fidelium," the Faith of the Catholic Church, as preserved and defined by her bishops in communion with Peter. This does not mean that we must stop thinking. Not at all. The mysteries of divine love are infinite, and will always need to be penetrated more deeply, unfolded more completely, and expressed more clearly for every generation. Within the parameters of a faith loyal to the Magisterium, in fact, there are a variety of ways of doing that theological task, whether it is the way of the Augustinian, the Franciscan, the Dominican, or the Jesuit. But whichever path we choose, it means that we must no longer think as individuals, but as members of a Body, in, with, and for that Body, and the visible head of that Body is Peter.

Let us continue with the "straight talk," for we are indeed dying men and women.

After honest reflection and prayer, if you are still not convinced by the case for the Petrine Ministry, then I have some questions for you.

First, who is it, in your world, who is able to speak the Gospel challenge to the whole Church and the whole of mankind? For if Jesus Christ is truly risen and living in His Church, His Mystical Body and Bride, His voice must be able to be heard today loud and clear, above the din of worldly voices — even if His Word is continually rejected by the world. You might answer: the World Council of Churches; here is the voice of the Body of Christ sounding out above the clamour. But do you really believe it? I am glad the World Council exists, for it is a good thing that Christians remain in dialogue with one another, and cooperate with one another as much as possible. In the same way, I am glad that the United Nations exists, which, for all its foibles, is still a format for dialogue and cooperation, where possible. But the World Council hardly sounds out loud and clear with the Gospel of Jesus Christ. It does not even claim to be an authoritative teaching body. Its ecumenical dialogue statements for example, tend to be vague and elusive, to keep everybody "on board." Its Eastern Orthodox members — the largest membership of any communion involved — are frequently disgruntled with its vague Faith-statements. The conservative Evangelicals don't participate. The Catholic presence in the Council is large, but we are not full members.

So where is the living, teaching voice of Jesus Christ, for the whole Church and the whole world? Is it in the Ecumenical Patriarchate in Constantinople? I am glad the Ecumenical Patriarchate exists, as a force for cohesion among the eastern churches, and a voice for most of the truths of Catholic Orthodoxy. But do most of the Eastern Orthodox churches look to Constantinople as the Pastor of pastors? I think not. Those who know Orthodoxy well know how jealously the other patriarchates guard their status and influence. The autocephalous-ethnic churches in particular are wary of Constantinople's pretensions, and it is difficult for the Ecumenical Patriarch to rally the Orthodox Churches to do anything, or to speak on anything as a united body. There is a "primacy of honor," in Constantinople, if you will, but not a universal pastorate.

What about in the Evangelical world? Of course, there have often been great evangelists who have wandered far and wide, preaching the basics of the Gospel message to the world. Personally, I think Billy Graham is one of the greatest of these, and he has certainly brought many people closer to Jesus Christ over the years. But for every Billy Graham, it seems, there are at least as many tele-evangelist charlatans, and demagogues. Sadly, in the world of evangelism, it is sometimes one step backward for every step forward. Christ Jesus will always inspire great preachers of the Gospel, in every generation, and from various denominations, but none of those really will be able to speak the whole Gospel message to the whole Church and to the whole world, with an expectation of being heard.

Whether it be as a result of an accident of history, or divine Providence, therefore, I would argue — and I would guess many Christians would agree — that the spiritual leader of Christianity at this moment of history is still the Bishop of Rome, presently Pope John Paul II. You may not always agree with him, but he is the only one who is in a position to exercise a nearly universal pastorate among Christians: responding to the issues facing Christians everywhere, addressing the whole Church and the whole world with the Gospel message. He has done so in his many journeys around the world. He has done so before the United Nations on several occasions. He does so in his encyclicals such as "Veritatis Splendor" and "Evangelium Vitae." He has done so in his book *Crossing the Threshold of Hope*. He has done so in the new *Catechism of the Catholic Church*, probably the most extensive, official proclamation of Christian teaching in history.

Of course, you might be willing to accept that at this present stage of history, the Pope should be listened to respectfully as the general spiritual leader of all Christians — and yet you could still refuse to accept his universal pastoral jurisdiction, and the infallibility of his highest teaching office. You might hope instead that one day, in a coming "Great Church" somehow syncretizing all the Christian traditions into one, or in a spiritually renewed ecumenical federation of churches, the popes might be willing to accept a role as no more than respected spiritual spokesmen, and leave it at that.

Again, some "straight talk" for you: in your heart of hearts, do you really think there is much chance of these things happening? And have you thought through what the *consequences* might be for the Christian world if they *did* happen?

The Eastern Orthodox, for example, are deeply divided among themselves about the future of ecumenical dialogue, and a significant portion of the Orthodox faithful would never be willing to accept any new "syncretized Church" or "federation of churches," nor any reconciliation with Rome, that watered down the Orthodox Faith as they have received it. Any move toward such a thing would surely create a tragic split amongst eastern Christians, and multitudes would reject the new compromises.

Again, you may hope that a more "liberal" pope will one day occupy the See of St. Peter, and be willing to forget about ancient claims to universal jurisdiction and doctrinal infallibility. But again, any attempt to do so would probably set bishop against bishop, cardinal against cardinal, perhaps even pope against anti-pope (it has happened before). An unholy mess would be the most likely result.

Of course, I do not think that the papacy would ever advocate such a thing, or at least no pope would ever officially teach such a thing "ex cathedra," for he would be prevented from doing so by the Holy Spirit. However, a future pope might *act* in a grossly irresponsible way, and bring confusion and division upon the Church. (May God preserve us from such a turn of events!)

Finally, I would ask you to consider whether it is at all likely that the conservative Evangelical movement, and the more liberal mainline Protestant churches, will one day, in the foreseeable future, be reconciled to one another in the sense of finding a common core of faith on which they can agree, and unite in a single federation. And will that common core include the belief in the inerrancy of Scripture or not? The mere posing of the question should be enough to convince you that the chances of a great "rapprochement" here are nearly zero.

In short, the ecumenical movement now may have reached something of an impasse. We have come a long way. Thanks be to God we have greater mutual understanding and tolerance, and greater cooperation in some areas than ever before. But the movement towards greater spiritual and visible unity among Christians was bound to stall at some point, simply because some of the divisions between Christian traditions are not just the result of misunderstanding, or a failure to synthesize complementary doctrines. Unfortunately, some of the divisions are based upon *irreconcilable, mutually contradictory truth-claims*. I will not try to enumerate all of these for you, but certainly they include issues such as the nature of scriptural and papal authority, the nature of priesthood and the ordained ministry, the role of the Blessed Virgin Mary in God's plan of salvation, and the nature of the presence of Christ in the Eucharist. Perhaps even more troublesome, there is an irreconcilable division that cuts across almost every major denomination today between, on the one hand, those who believe that we are called to preserve, expound and spread a specific gospel of "good tidings," guaranteed for us by the authority of the incarnate Word and His apostles, the Scriptures and the Church; or, on the other hand, those who cannot accept any fully trustworthy revelatory authorities, relying instead solely on the Spirit and their own subjective powers of reasoning to uncover from the "husks" of the Christian tradition a few "kernels" of truth about God and man, and some principles of moral idealism. The chasm that separates these two positions — the *objectivism* of historic Christianity, and the *subjectivism* of "liberal modernism" — is, I believe impossible to span, and the disintegration of the worldwide Anglican communion along these lines in recent decades is, quite possibly, a grim portent of the future for other churches.

In short, those who are waiting for a new universal federation of churches, much less the syncretized "Great Church" that Protestant ecumenists dreamed about early in the 20th century, are liable to be waiting a very long time indeed.

Of course, that must raise the question: just what is the Church of Jesus Christ, if it cannot ever seem to recover the unity for which our Lord so earnestly prayed before His passion? After nearly 1,000 years of schism, regrouping, and schism again, the world can be partially forgiven for turning something of a deaf ear to those evangelists who claim that they come from the churches with a gospel of "reconciliation" to proclaim!

The true Church of Jesus Christ, however, is ever the same: the very Body and Bride of the living Lord. And if the Church is His Body and Bride, then always it must be *one social and spiritual organism*. A body cannot live and work with its limbs and organs dismembered: "apart from me you can do nothing" (Jn. 15:5). If the Church really is, as St. Paul taught, the one "Body of Christ" (I Cor. 12:27) and "the pillar and ground of the truth" (I Tim. 3:15), then it is impossible for it to be divided up into local churches that significantly disagree with each other on matters of revealed doctrine (Eph. 4:5; I Cor. 1:10), or that lack bonds of governmental fellowship (Rom. 12:4-5) or bonds of sacramental communion (I Cor. 10:17). The true Church must ever be one in worship, government and doctrine. Otherwise, the "powers of death" have prevailed against her despite our Lord's promise (Mt. 16:18), and she does not fully manifest the unity of the Trinitarian life of God, despite our Lord's earnest prayer (Jn. 17:11). But the Church in its Catholic fullness is one, and always has been. She has suffered wounds, to be sure. Some of these wounds she has helped to inflict upon herself by the sins of her own members — but she lives still. As St. Ambrose once said: "where Peter is, there is the Church." And Peter is in Rome.

POSTSCRIPT: AN OLIVE BRANCH FROM THE EAST?

As this book was being prepared for publication, a significant work on the papacy by an Eastern Orthodox theologian made its first appearance in an English translation: *You are Peter: An Orthodox Reflection on the Exercise of Papal Primacy*, by Olivier Clément (New City Press, 2003). In many respects, this is an admirable volume. Clément takes the reader on a rapid tour of the history of the exercise of papal primacy. Along the way, he presents his own, fairly irenic understanding of the Petrine Ministry, including a plea for a closer union between East and West that does not involve capitulation by either side regarding the proper role of the See of Rome. Conspicuous by its absence from this book is the old line of Eastern apologetics that Rome never possessed more than a primacy of "honor" in the ancient church. In fact, Clément blames both East and West for developing truncated versions of ecclesiology during the second Christian millennium: Rome exaggerated the authority of its ancient primacy, while the Byzantines tried to forget about Rome's ancient primacy altogether. Clément's book comes with a glowing forward by Cardinal Avery Dulles, S.J., who sees in this volume a fulfillment of Pope John Paul II's earnest desire for a new dialogue with the East: putting aside the polemics of the past, and seeking "to find a way of exercising the [papal] primacy which, while in no way renouncing what is essential to its mission, is nonetheless open to a new situation ("Ut Unum Sint," 95).

Clearly, Olivier Clément's book marks a step forward in ecumenical dialogue on these matters. Nevertheless, it is only a small step. There is much that calls for comment and correction in his short volume. Despite Clément's good intentions, scholarly acumen, and peaceable vision for East-West reconciliation, the book would seem to fall well short of Pope John Paul II's plea that ecumenical reconciliation should not be pursued at the expense of truth ("Ut Unum Sint," 36).

A Truncated History

To begin with, Clément's survey of the history of the papacy is marred by numerous shortcomings. For example, he makes only passing mention of the writings of St. Clement of Rome and St. Ireneus of Lyons, yet these are the two earliest witnesses we possess (1st and 2nd century respectively) to Christian belief in the universal appellate jurisdiction and trustworthy teaching authority of the See of Rome. Clément quotes St. Cyprian of Carthage that Jesus gave to all the apostles "equal power," yet he makes no mention of the deeds and letters of St. Cyprian that indicate a somewhat different perspective. Clément writes: "It is only with Callistus (around 220) or perhaps Victor (192-194) that the bishops of Rome base their primacy on the words of Jesus in Matthew 16:13-19, and especially on those in Luke 22:31-32, and Jn. 21:15-18."[29] However, the fact is that we have no record of Roman preeminence being challenged prior to Pope St. Victor, and therefore there was no occasion for Rome to appeal to its Petrine foundation to justify the exercise of its authority prior to that pontificate. Clément laments the "regrettable" fact that "the importance of Paul in defining the primacy of Rome diminished little by little until, in the sixteenth century ... Rome denounced as heretical all those who stressed the equality of Peter and Paul."[30] But this

---

[29] Olivier Clément, *You are Peter* (Hyde Park, NY: New City Press, 2003), 28

[30] Ibid., 37.

development only stands to reason: after all, to whom did Jesus give the "keys" of the kingdom? Who was named by our Lord "the Rock" of the Church, and the shepherd of His whole flock? Peter or Paul?

Much of Cléments book centers on the period of the ancient ecumenical councils. Yet here again, we are presented with a truncated version of the real story. For example, Clément writes:

> An important, while not ecumenical council at Serdica (343-344) defined, to the benefit of Rome and of the universal Church, a law not exactly of appeal but of abrogation: the pope could refuse the evidence of a bishop and send "presbyters from among his entourage" to participate in the appeal judgment rendered by neighboring bishops of the province where the dispute arose. With time these canons were accepted in the East … ."[31]

What Clément fails to tell the reader is that he is reporting an Eastern version and interpretation of the canons of Serdica which has always been disputed by the West. The Western version and interpretation acknowledges the authority of the Bishop of Rome to hear appeals and hold retrials in Rome itself — and there are several reasons for thinking that in this case, the Western interpretation is correct. First of all, at the end of the first century, when St. Clement of Rome received an appeal from Corinth, and intervened to restore the clergy to their posts (see above, Chapter II), he did not merely send "presbyters from among his entourage" to participate in an appeal judgment rendered by local bishops! Rather, he *ordered* the restoration of the clergy in Corinth, evidently reserving the right to do so on the basis of the appellate jurisdiction of the See of Rome. Moreover, the Council of Serdica (343-344 A.D.) evidently did not intend to

---

[31] Ibid., 34.

condemn the kind of intervention made by Pope St. Julius in the dispute over the See of Alexandria (341-342 A.D.) — and again, Pope St. Julius did not just send presbyters to participate in a local retrial! Rather, Pope St. Julius summoned St. Athanasius of Alexandria to Rome, abrogated the deposition of Athanasius, ordered that he be restored to his See and rendered judgment upon the penitent malefactors in the affair in Rome. We saw a somewhat similar procedure utilized by Pope St. Gregory the Great in his dispute with the Patriarch of Constantinople, John the Faster, in 593 A.D. (Chapter III above). Gregory ordered that a retrial of accused presbyters from Constantinople should take place in Rome itself, because, he wrote, even that patriarch is "subject to the Apostolic See." Constantinople acquiesced in this procedure.

In short, it is evident that Rome *always* reserved the right to act as the highest court of appeal in disciplinary and jurisdictional disputes. Serdica did not grant to the papacy a new (and only very limited) authority to exercise appellate jurisdiction over distant churches. Serdica stated that while Rome "may" send arbiters to take part in local retrials in distant places, "it is in the power of the bishop [of Rome] to do whatever seems right to him" in such cases. (In some cases, it would be preferable for Rome to authorize a local re-trial, with Roman legates present, simply because of the impracticalities involved in bringing all the parties in a dispute all the way to Rome.) The optional appellate procedures outlined at Serdica, therefore, supplement the long-standing claim of the Roman See to have the "final word" in such disputes, but do not contradict that claim. In the cases of Pope St. Clement, Pope St. Julius, and Pope St. Gregory the Great, their exercise of Roman appellate jurisdiction was widely (though not unanimously) accepted by the Eastern episcopate at the time.

Clément tells us that at the first council in Constantinople (the Second Ecumenical Council) in 381 A.D., "the primacy of Rome was considered simply as a primacy of honor because of the political importance of Rome as a city (canon 3)."[32] Actually, the canon passed by that council states only that the See of Constantinople has special importance because it is "New Rome" (that is, because it is the new imperial capital), but nothing at all is said explicitly about the basis or nature of the primacy of Old Rome — a primacy which the Council reaffirmed *despite the fact that Old Rome was no longer the capital city of the empire!* Obviously, this canon could be read as implying the importance of imperial status as a factor in all claims of primatial authority — which is why Pope St. Damasus responded to it with his famous "Decree," reasserting the *Petrine* basis of Roman Primacy (a decree which was not contested by any saint or Father of the ancient Church). But it is not true to say that the Council accorded to Old Rome a mere imperial "primacy of honor."

Of the Third Ecumenical Council (431 A.D.) Clément writes: "The Council of Ephesus condemned Nestorius out of the fullness of its own authority. Its considerations were based not on the letter of the pope (who claimed to have settled the matter) but on that of Cyril of Alexandria."[33] What Clément omits here is that St. Cyril presided over this council with the permission and encouragement of Pope Celestine, whose legates at the Council acknowledged and supported Cyrillian orthodoxy.

Of the Fourth Ecumenical Council (Chalcedon, 451 A.D.), Clément gives the reader barely half the story. He writes:

> Chalcedon saw a new affirmation of the council's self-sufficiency, of its being complete in itself. ... The message of

---

[32] Ibid., 42
[33] Ibid., 42-43.

> Pope Leo, his celebrated "Tome," was only received by the
> council after long and detailed examination. It was then seen
> to be an expression of the common faith, "it is the teaching
> of the apostles ... the teaching of Cyril," "the orthodox
> faith," "Peter speaking through the mouth of Leo."[34]

However, it is clear that there was already a large pro-Leonine party among the assembled Eastern bishops even before the completion of any "long and detailed examination" of the Tome. That is why when Bishop Peter of Corinth crossed over to their side to join them, he was greeted with the shout "Peter thinks as does Peter: orthodox bishop welcome!" In other words, the Eastern bishops were divided among themselves. Some evidently accepted St. Leo's Tome because it had been issued with the full Petrine authority of Rome, and therefore expressed the orthodox Faith. Other Eastern bishops would not accept it until they had thoroughly examined the document and found it in accord with the orthodox Faith as they understood it. In short, at Chalcedon we see the deference of the East to Roman primacy, but no clear consensus as to how far that deference should go. The letter written by the Eastern Patriarchs to Pope St. Leo after the Council, seeking his approval, seems deferential in the extreme to the See of Rome (see Chapter III, above). How, then, can Clément legitimately claim that Chalcedon manifested "a new affirmation of the council's self-sufficiency, of its being complete in itself?"

Clément's treatment of the Fifth Ecumenical Council (Constantinople II, 551-552 A.D.) is also inadequate. Clément writes:

> At the fifth ecumenical council (Constantinople II) the Fathers
> were involved in the discussion of the "Three Chapters"
> despite the ban of the pope who, although present at
> Constantinople, refused to participate in the council. From the

---

[34] Ibid., 43

outset the council stated that a question of faith could only be resolved collegially, by a synod, and not by a single individual, not even by the pope. …[35]

At Constantinople II, Pope Vigilius, having arrived in the capital, refused either to take part in the council or to join in the condemnation of certain texts that he considered orthodox, whereupon the council declared that he was excluded from the catholic communion, and his name was erased from the records. But six months after the end of the council, Vigilius recognized it, and his successors did likewise. So it was that the popes and the entire Church, both in the West and in the East, acknowledged the ecumenical legitimacy of a council that excommunicated a pope because he had opposed it[36]

There are significant omissions from this account of Constantinople II. First of all, Pope Vigilius originally "arrived" in Constantinople because he had been taken there by force by the Byzantine Emperor Justinian, to compel his consent to imperial ecclesiastical policy. In fact, this whole council of Eastern bishops operated under a thinly veiled threat of coercion by the Emperor — which may account for their bold, insulting treatment of the Pope, after Justinian's example! Secondly, Rome subsequently "acknowledged" the ecumenical legitimacy of the theological formulas of this council, but did not ever explicitly endorse the so-called "excommunication" of Vigilius. Rome had already endorsed two previous councils as "ecumenical" (Constantinople I, and Chalcedon) without ratifying every act or canon of those councils.

Concerning the Sixth Ecumenical Council (Constantinople III, 680-681), Clément states:

The Fathers, restoring the unity of the Church, anathematized not only the patriarchs of Constantinople, Alexandria and Antioch, but also Pope Honorius: all dead by then, and all compromised in the monothelite controversy.

---

[35] Ibid., 43.
[36] Ibid., 47.

At the same council, the letter of Pope Agathon, his *suggestion (anaphora)* was respectfully introduced for debate, scrutinized, and only at the end received fully, because it was in accordance ... with the decisions of Chalcedon and the entire tradition: the gospels, apostles, councils ...[37]

Here again, this is hardly the full story. As a matter of fact, (1) Rome never received or accepted the act of this Council that condemned Pope Honorius as a monothelite heretic (see Chapter V above). Moreover, (2) even if Honorius was a heretic, this would be no mark against the teaching authority of the Apostolic See. The Catholic Church does not claim that it is impossible for a pope to hold — or even to express to a limited audience — heretical viewpoints. For example, in the 14th century Pope John XXII preached an heretical sermon at St. John Lateran in Rome, and his doctrine was formally condemned by his successor Pope Benedict XII in the dogmatic constitution "Benedictus Deus" (1336). What the Catholic Church has always believed, however, is that the Bishop of Rome is preserved by the Holy Spirit from proclaiming and defining error in matters and faith and morals whenever he addresses the universal Church as pastor and teacher. (3) Finally, even Clément admits elsewhere in his book that there was a significant group of Eastern bishops at this Council who believed that "Rome possessed by the will of God, a real Petrine ministry with a certain primacy of jurisdiction. Therefore, Peter spoke in a privileged way through Agathon, because Agathon was his successor and Vicar." [38] As at Chalcedon two centuries earlier, here again we see the divided mind of the Eastern episcopate on the nature of the Roman Primacy.

There are further difficulties with Clément's understanding of the development of the papacy in the medieval era, as well as with his exposition of the teachings of Vatican

---

[37] Ibid., 44.
[38] Ibid., 50-51.

I and II. However, it would be pointless to set out these difficulties in detail. They will be evident to anyone who reads Clément's book in contrast with this present volume.

One more aspect of Clément's version of ecclesiastical history, however, should not be passed over without comment. Unfortunately, Clément cannot tell his story without including a litany of the moral crimes committed by Catholics against Eastern Orthodox Christians. This includes the sack of Constantinople by the western crusaders in 1204, the "exploitation" of the Byzantine world by the merchants of Venice, the Catholic "Uniate" missions, and the massacre of tens of thousands of Serbs by Croat Catholics during the second world war. Few would dispute these facts. What is sad — and sadly typical of Orthodox polemics — is that this litany of Western crimes against the East is offered *with no mention at all of the crimes committed by Christians of the East against Catholics of the West.* No mention of the collaboration of portions of the Orthodox hierarchy with the suppression of Catholicism by the communist regimes of Eastern Europe (e.g., in Romania); no mention of the centuries of oppression suffered by Polish and Ukranian Catholics under the heel of the Tsars of Russia; no mention either of the massacre of Latin Christians in the city of Constantinople in 1182 — just a few years prior to the infamous "sacking" of that city by the crusaders. In short, Western and Eastern Christians, given the opportunity, have wronged each other for the better part of 1,000 years. It is tendentious, and counter-productive, to recite the sins of one side while remaining silent about the sins of the other.

An Idealistic Ecclesiology

The heart of Clément's book is found in the chapter entitled, "A Creative Tension." Here he offers the reader more than just an Eastern view of the history of the papacy; he offers us an ecclesiological paradigm, an ideal which he believes was on display in the ancient church:

> The true greatness of the period of the ecumenical councils is precisely that the power of decision [that is, regarding matters of faith, morals, and jurisdiction] rested with no one; neither pope, nor council, nor emperor, nor public feeling. All thought that they had the final word, which meant that no one had it except, rightly, the Holy Spirit. ... It is our task today, going beyond the words ... to reflect on the lived ecclesial experience of a period when, through compromise and miracles, tensions were resolved throughout the greater part of Christendom ... [through] the free communion of personal consciences in the Holy Spirit.[39]

Here, indeed, is a noble ideal: final authority in the Church should reside in the free consent and accord of pope, council, clergy and laity together, by the Holy Spirit. This was certainly the view of many Eastern hierarchs from the fifth century onward. On the other hand, it was never really the view of the West, nor the view of some of the greatest saints and Fathers of the East. Moreover, the result of the ascendancy of this viewpoint in the East was the lasting schism of Egypt and Syria, and then a schism with Rome that could not be successfully resolved even in ecumenical council. Only the West fully realized — along with St. Athanasius, St. Cyril of Alexandria, Bl. Theodoret, St. Flavian, St. Maximus the Confessor, and St. Theodore the Studite — that in a church in which "wheat" and "weeds" ever grow together (Mt. 13:24-30), a universal primate with sufficient authority is needed to keep the universal Church in the unity of faith and communion. Moreover, it was the West (along with these saints of the East) which fully realized that Jesus Christ had foreseen this problem, and provided a sufficient remedy for it, in the Petrine Ministry.

---

[39] Ibid., 57-58.

Clément cites the great medieval philosopher Nicholas of Cusa as a proponent of his ideal:

> [Nicholas] took it upon himself to recall the heart of Western Christendom to the authentic tradition of the Church. He refused to decide who, whether pope or council, should be superior to the other. The ideal to be pursued was agreement between the two. In case of disagreement, the important thing was to know "on which side lay the support of the universal church." It is not a relationship of authority or submission, either in one direction or the other, valid in all circumstances. Only the Church could attest the ecclesiality of pope or council.[40]

The problem is that the great Nicholas of Cusa seems to have *repudiated* this idealistic viewpoint later in his life, precisely because he lived long enough to see its failure in the western conciliarist movement of the 15th century. Conciliarism, and the ideal of universal "reception" (see Chapter IV above), led to ecclesiastical division and paralysis. Nicholas eventually became a papist — and a cardinal.

In his chapter entitled "The Mystery of Primacy," Clément argues that the Church is most fully herself when "tensions are held in balance without predetermined juridical solutions ... where tensions are held in balance, even in robust confrontations like that between Peter and Paul at Antioch, the last word belongs to none but the Holy Spirit, who cannot but bring forth agreement — a certitude of faith for all who put their confidence in the promises of Christ."[41] Yet the reader cannot help but notice that the very historical facts that Clément relates throughout his book disproves his own ideal. A Church which has no *universally* recognized, Christ-given pastoral ministry with supreme teaching and juridical authority simply does *not* "bring forth agreement" or "certitude of

---

[40] Ibid., 62.
[41] Ibid., 94.

faith." The Holy Spirit has evidently failed to bring forth such spontaneous agreement between East and West for more than a thousand years, leading many to wonder, and endlessly debate, precisely where the "certitude of faith" might lie in regard to the doctrines of the Holy Trinity, Purgatory, the Immaculate Conception, and even the morality of divorce. Even in the late patristic era, which Clément idealizes, this ecclesiology simply did not work. Clément writes:

> For its part the council could not prevent the tearing asunder of the Church in the ancient Christian lands of Egypt and Syria in the fifth and sixth centuries. Clearly, the dogma of Chalcedon was an immense accomplishment ... but how can one forget all those bishops in the Middle East who claimed that the new definition ran counter to Tradition? Philoxenus of Mabbug, for example, who was no heedless theologian of little consequence, disputed the claim that the council had been "received" by the entire Church, a reception which alone, for him, would have obliged acceptance of its decisions. Who was right, one might naively ask?[42]

No, it is not a naïve question: it is a perfectly reasonable question to ask if we are being encouraged to believe (as Clément insists) that the apostolic hierarchy of the Church cannot be known to have made binding judgments on matters of faith and morals in the Holy Spirit without the subsequent "reception" of their decisions by the Church at large, "the free communion of personal consciences" (cf. Acts 15:28) — a reception which, of course, is nearly impossible to measure! Surely, on Clément's view, Philip of Mabbug's opposition to the authority of Chalcedon was entirely right, just as, on Clément's view, Mark of Ephesus was entirely within his rights when he left the 15th century Council of Florence early, in order to stir up opposition to that Council's decision among the Byzantine monks and laity, thus ensuring that what had

---

[42] Ibid., 56-57.

been agreed unanimously by the bishops of the East and West at Florence would not be "received" back home. In short, the schism with Egypt and Syria in the fifth and sixth centuries, which lasted 1500 years, and the continuation of the schism with Rome after Florence — both of these tragic divisions in the Body of Christ are largely the direct result of the flawed ecclesiology of well-intentioned Christian leaders of the East such as Philip of Mabbug, and Mark of Ephesus. Clément's ecclesiology only repeats their mistakes. The view of the Catholic Church is much simpler: a council can be known to possess a truly "ecumenical" authority when it is recognized and received as such by the universal pastorate, the See of St. Peter. If such admirable men as Philip and Mark, and their followers, had properly understood and accepted the trustworthy teaching authority of the "key-bearing" Rock and Shepherd of the universal Church — the Petrine Primacy that Jesus had established — they would never have fallen into schism, nor led others into schism. The unity of the Church in truth and communion would have been preserved.

Olivier Clément's invitation to Catholics seems charitable and peaceable enough. He is saying to us, in effect: "Let us return to what we all generally believed about papal primacy in the first millennium, and forget about medieval and modern developments as regrettable errors. In the second millennium Rome 'arrogated' to itself universal jurisdiction and infallibility, while the East generally fell into 'amnesia' about the ancient, universal, pastoral role of the Petrine Ministry. Let us leave behind both arrogance and amnesia. Let us be reconciled in the Holy Spirit after the pattern of the ancient, undivided Church."

A Catholic who knows the historical facts, however, simply cannot accept Clément's invitation. As we have seen,

other than St. Firmillian and St. Cyprian (and there are significant ambiguities in the writings of the latter) in the first
eight Christian centuries no saint or Father of the Church,
East or West, denied that Rome was the center of the universal communion of the Churches, or that Rome properly possessed at least appellate jurisdiction in the universal Church,
or that Rome was the trustworthy touchstone and reference
point of the authentic Catholic Faith. Some of the ancient
Fathers believed and taught these things explicitly. Thus, the
ancient ideal, according to the saints and Fathers — in
accord with a reasonable exigesis of the Petrine texts in the
New Testament — leans very much in favor of the Catholic
view. It is true that many of the bishops and patriarchs of the
East sometimes lapsed from this ancient consensus (e.g., in
the Acacian schism in the late 5th century, or at the Second
Council of Constantinople in 551-552 AD). But these lapses
can be explained by the pressure put upon them by the imperial authorities (e.g., Byzantine Emperors such as Zeno and
Justinian). In any case the Eastern saints and Fathers did not
have much part in these deviations.

What Clément is really asking Catholics to do is to
embrace an ecclesiology of universal "reception" which,
wherever and whenever it has gained some currency in the
Church, has clearly shown that it does not "work" in unifying the Church in faith or communion. The cases of Philip of
Mabbug and Mark of Ephesus (discussed above) are instruc-
tive in this regard.

In fact, what Clément is asking us to do is to jettison the
one thing that the Catholic world has to offer the Orthodox
communion of the East which can overcome the ethnic and
national divisions which weaken and paralyze it: namely,
obedience, in proper measure, to the universal pastorate that

Jesus gave to us in the See of Peter. When a Catholic looks at the Orthodox communion of churches today, he finds much that attracts him, and much that does not. Can anyone deny that the Orthodox communion is chronically wounded, and in many ways paralyzed in its missionary outreach, and its prophetic social witness, by the ethnic, national, and jurisdictional divisions which continually plague it? At the same time, its ecclesial life is spiritually nourished and sustained by the Lord Jesus in the Eucharist, the glorious Eastern liturgy, and the mystical wisdom of the Eastern saints. These latter gifts from the Holy Spirit need not be lost in a restored communion with Rome. Rather, these are precisely the gifts that the Eastern Christians must bring with them into the re-union, because they are precisely the areas where their western brethren are weaker, and in need of help!

Toward Re-union

This brings us to one final criticism of Clément's book. Unfortunately, Clément's book is yet another discussion of the papacy by an Eastern Orthodox writer that almost completely ignores the witness of the "black sheep" of the Orthodox family: the 19th century Russian philosopher and theologian Vladimir Soloviev. What Clément invites us to seek is a compromise between East and West regarding the Petrine Ministry: a kind of "Via Media" solution allegedly rooted in the patristic era. For Soloviev, on the other hand, there is no place for compromise. The East needs to embrace the fullness of the Petrine Ministry in order to save itself from its ethnic and national divisions, its weaknesses, and its excessive otherworldliness. At the same time, the Catholic world desperately needs the fullness of all that the East would bring to the reunion, especially her rich traditions of liturgy and spirituality. Soloviev wrote in *The Russian Church and the Papacy:*

For centuries the monks of the holy mountain of Athos, true representatives of the isolated Eastern church, have spent all their energies in prayer and the contemplation of the uncreated light of Tabor. They are perfectly right: prayer and the contemplation of uncreated things are essential to the Christian life. But can we allow that this occupation of the soul constitutes the *whole* Christian life? For that is what we must do if we try to put the Orthodox East, with its peculiar character and special religious tendencies, in the place of the universal Church. We have in the East a church at prayer, but where among us is the Church in action, asserting itself as a spiritual force absolutely independent of the powers of the world? Where in the East is the Church of the living God, the Church which in every generation legislates for mankind, which establishes and develops the formulation of eternal truth with which to counteract the continually changing forms of error? Where is the Church which labors to remold the whole social life of the nations in accordance with the Christian ideal, and to guide them toward the supreme goal of Creation — free and perfect union with the Creator? ...

We must above all recognize the insufficiency of our traditional religious ideal, and make a sincere attempt to realize a more complete conception of Christianity. There is no need to invent or create anything new for this purpose. We merely have to restore to our religion its catholic or universal character by recognizing our oneness with the active part of the Christian world, with the West centralized and organized for a universal activity and possessing all that we lack. We are not asked to change our nature as Easterns or to repudiate the specific character of our religious genius. We have only to recognize unreservedly the elementary truth that we of the East are but a part of the universal Church, a part moreover which has not its center within itself, and that, therefore, it behooves us to restore the link between our individual forces on the circumference and the great universal center which Providence has placed in the West[43]

On the part of the Catholic Church, there are certainly reforms that could be made in the exercise of the Petrine

---

[43] Vladimir Soloviev, *The Russian Church and the Papacy* (San Diego: Catholic Answers, 2001), 53-54.

Ministry that would more clearly manifest its proper role, without compromising its essential mission. For example, the Apostolic See does not claim to be the source of each and every bishop's divine commission to shepherd the People of God (Chapter III, above). In fact, the "apostolic succession" of ministry is imparted at each bishop's *consecration,* not when that bishop is acknowledged by Rome. Thus, as Clément writes, "it is in no way essential to the exercise of [the Petrine] primacy that the Bishop of Rome should appoint the bishops of the entire world."[44] The general pattern in the ancient church was for each diocese to choose its own bishop. Episcopal consecration would be bestowed by bishops from the neighboring dioceses, while the canonical mission of the new bishop to shepherd a particular diocese would need to be recognized and ratified by the regional patriarchate, as well as by Rome. This ancient pattern might be more widely restored.

There might also be a reform of the exercise of the papal Magisterium. While the authentic exercise of the infallible "extraordinary" teaching authority of the See of St. Peter is not subject to subsequent approval or ratification by the college of bishops, nevertheless (according to the official Roman commentary on the decrees of the First Vatican Council), the pope is morally bound to consult with the leading bishops and theologians of the Church, before issuing an infallible definition of faith or morals (Chapter IV above). Moreover, while he is not bound to echo their majority view, he certainly must not contradict any *consensus* that he finds there. The historical record shows that the papacy was careful to undertake such broad consultations before defining the Immaculate Conception and the Assumption of the Blessed Virgin Mary as articles of Faith. Today, these moral obliga-

---

[44] Ibid., 92.

tions could be given some canonical form: for example, the Pope could be required to make every reasonable effort to consult with the Congregation for the Doctrine of the Faith, the College of Cardinals, and (in a re-united Church) with the Eastern Patriarchs before issuing an infallible definition. Such a canonical requirement would hardly block the effective exercise of the extraordinary papal Magisterium, nor would it violate the principles laid down by Vatican I and II. It would simply provide the See of St. Peter with proper guidelines for carrying out its moral obligation to listen before it speaks, and to gather the very best reflections of its brother bishops and learned theologians in the Holy Spirit before pronouncing a solemn judgment. Pope John Paul II has taught (in *"Tertio Millenio Adveniente"*) that "obedience" and "consultation" are two of the hallmarks of the exercise of authentic pastoral ministry in the Church. They can also be seen as two of the marks of the prudent exercise of the extraordinary papal Magisterium.

Perhaps it was reforms such as these that Pope John Paul II had in mind when he expressed his desire in *"Ut Unum Sint"* for a new dialogue on the exercise of papal primacy. Olivier Clément's book is a relatively charitable attempt to engage in such a dialogue. Nevertheless, as we have seen, reconciliation between the East and the Catholic world on the issue of the Petrine Ministry cannot happen in the way that Clément suggests. His ideal of an endlessly unresolvable "creative tension" in the Church between the papacy, the college of bishops, and the wider Church is a recipe for schism, confusion, and ecclesiastical paralysis — as the history of Christendom sadly attests. Nor will reconciliation between Catholicism and the East come by the abandonment of the teachings on the Petrine Primacy of

Vatican I and Vatican II. Such a strategy would not amount to a *reform* of the exercise of the Petrine Ministry, but a direct *repudiation* of it as it has always been received and accepted, implicitly or explicitly, by the Catholic Church, including some of the greatest saints and Fathers of the East. On the other hand, while Vatican I and II cannot be repudiated, the principles laid down at these councils might be further unfolded, elucidated, and applied in the ways suggested in this "Postscript." At the same time, Catholic Christians continue to hope and pray that our Eastern Orthodox brothers and sisters will make every effort to embrace a reasonable and comprehensive exigesis of the "Petrine texts" in the New Testament, and will listen more comprehensively to the ancient consensus of the saints and the Fathers regarding the indispensable, unifying authority of the See of St. Peter.

SUGGESTIONS FOR FURTHER READING

Karl Adam, *The Spirit of Catholicism*. London, Sheed and Ward, 1938. A classic exposition of the distinctively Catholic understanding of the Church as the Body of Christ, the Petrine Ministry, the sacraments, and the process of salvation.

James Likoudis, *The Divine Primacy of the Bishop of Rome and Modern Eastern Orthodoxy*. No publisher listed, 2002. Available only from the author at credo.stormloader.com.

J. Michael Miller, C.S.B., *The Shepherd and the Rock*. Our Sunday Visitor Press, 1995. Very good on the contemporary structure and operations of the Holy See.

Pope Pius XII, Encyclical Letter, "Mystici Corporis," (The Mystical Body of Christ), 1943.

Joseph Cardinal Ratzinger, *Called to Communion: Understanding the Church Today*. San Francisco, Ignatius Press, 1996.

Stephen K. Ray, *Upon this Rock*. San Francisco, Ignatius Press, 1999. Very good source for quotations and analysis of the early Fathers on the Petrine Primacy.

OF SPECIAL INTEREST:

Adriano Garuti, O.F.M., *Primacy of the Bishop of Rome and the Ecumenical Dialogue*. San Francisco, Ignatius Press, 2004.

This book is a very thorough review of all the ongoing ecumenical discussions regarding the role of the papacy – a vital resource for in-depth theological research on this subject.

The reader will be surprised to discover the importance that Eastern Orthodox theologians in ecumenical dialogue attribute to the Apostolic Constitutions (a late 4th century collection of canons by Julian the Arian, based in part on the apocryphal letter of Clement to James, and on the regional councils of Antioch and Laodicea), especially to canon 34:

> The bishops of every region ought to know who is the first (protos) among them, and so esteem him as their head and not do any great thing without his consent; but every one ought to manage only the affairs that belong to his own diocese and the territory subject to it. But let him [i.e., the first one] not do anything without the consent of all the other [bishops]; for it is by this means that there will be unanimity, and God will be glorified through Christ in the Holy Spirit.

According to many Orthodox theologians, "re-establishment of full communion will be possible only when Catholics recognize this model" (Garuti, p. 72).

I am not sure what is to be gained by an appeal to this ancient canon with regard to the Petrine Primacy. First of all, the Apostolic Constitutions are of somewhat dubious origin; they are not traceable to the early Fathers, nor to the ancient Ecumenical Councils, but compiled by an Arian, in part from an apocryphal document, and two regional synods. Secondly, and more importantly, canon 34 discusses the nature of regional primacy, which in most cases is an ecclesial creation, based on geographical, demographic, and even political circumstances. The Petrine Ministry, on the other hand, is not just a regional primacy "writ large": it is of divine institution, based on a direct commission from Jesus Christ Himself, with unique responsibilities and prerogatives. Ancient canons related to regional primacy, therefore, are not simply transferable to discussions of the universal, uniquely Petrine Primacy. In fact, other early canonical documents of the Eastern Church paint a very different picture of patriarchal authority – and especially of the authority of the See of St. Peter. James Likoudis explains (*The Divine Primacy of the Bishop of Rome*, 2002 edition, p. 113-114):

> I would refer you to the Arabic canons attributed to the Council of Nicea which were incorporated into the collections of the ancient Syrian, Coptic, Ethiopian, and Melkite Churches. These 73 pseudo-Nicene canons can be traced back to the 5th century, and reflect the original acceptance of the Roman Primacy among the Christians of the East. Among these canons we read:
>
> > "It is the will of this ecumenical synod that for all things which have not been justly conducted by a metropolitan or other bishop,

the patriarch has the power to decide by his own authority. For he is found above his fellows and all the bishops are sons of his heritage. The honor of metropolitans is like that of an elder brother who finds himself among his brothers. The honor of a patriarch [on the other hand] is thus of a father who has authority over his children. And as the patriarch has the power to do all that he wishes for good in the dominion of his authority, so he of Rome will have power over all the patriarchs like Blessed Peter over the entire community. For he has likewise the place of Peter in the Church of Rome."